postmodern fables

The publication of this book was assisted by a bequest from Josiah H. Chase to honor his parents, Ellen Rankin Chase and Josiah Hook Chase, Minnesota territorial pioneers.

postmodern fables

Jean-François Lyotard

Translated by Georges Van Den Abbeele

University of Minnesota Press

Minneapolis

London

The University of Minnesota Press gratefully acknowledges
financial assistance provided by the French Ministry of
Culture for the translation of this book.

Originally published in French as *Moralités postmodernes*, © 1993
Éditions Galilée, Paris.

Published by the University of Minnesota Press
111 Third Avenue South, Suite 290
Minneapolis, MN 55401-2520
http://www.upress.umn.edu

Printed in the United States of America on acid-free paper

Library of Congress Cataloging-in-Publication Data

Lyotard, Jean François.
      [Moralités postmodernes. English]
      Postmodern fables / Jean-François Lyotard ; translated by
Georges Van Den Abbeele.
          p.   cm.
      Includes bibliographical references and index.
      ISBN 0-8166-2554-9 (hc : alk. paper)
      1. Ethics, Modern—20th century.   2. Postmodernism—
Moral and ethical aspects.   I. Title.
B2430.L963.M6713   1997
194—dc21   97-25953

Contents

Preface

After a short story, a fable or tale, sketch or *exemplum*, a moral draws out an unpretentious, localized, and provisional bit of wisdom, soon to be forgotten. Morals often, heedlessly, contradict each other. Together, they make a rustling of maxims, a cheerful lament: that's life.

Today, life is fast. It vaporizes morals. Futility suits the postmodern, for words as well as things. But that doesn't keep us from asking questions: how to live, and why? The answers are deferred. As they always are, of course. But this time, there is a semblance of knowing: that life is going every which way.

But do we know this? We represent it to ourselves rather. Every which way of life is flaunted, exhibited, enjoyed for the love of variety. The moral of all morals would be that of "aesthetic" pleasure.

Here, then, are fifteen notes on postmodern aestheticization. And against it! You're not done living because you chalk it up to artifice.

verbiages

chapter 1

Marie Goes to Japan

The *stream of cultural capital*?[1] But that's me, Marie tells herself, while watching the baggage return rotate at Narita airport. A little stream, but still a stream. Cultural, that's for sure, they buy culture from me. Capital too. I'm not the owner, thank God, nor the manager. Just a little cultural labor force they can exploit. But correctly, under contract, let me add, and with my signature. No great discovery here. Half wage earner, half craftsperson. That's how you wanted it. You rush around Europe, the continents, airplanes, faxes, telephones, mail to the four corners of the world. It's hard, really hard. Fun, but hard. Once, it was fun. And on top of it, you still have to work. You can't always sell the same product. You have to invent, read, imagine. Because without it, they're not happy, they'll say you're

---

1. In English in the original, as is also the case for the other italicized English words in this text.—Trans.

taking them for fools. Or else, that you're on the way out. You know, Marie, she has nothing else to say. Throw it in the trash.

If everything goes right, there's a hostess (I see her, that's who's coming, I'm sure of it) or some assistant who comes by the airport to give you a lift. A half hour at the hotel to freshen up. Sometimes, it's after eighteen hours of nonstop flying, huh? Cocktails and dinner, then the lecture and a drink. Or a cocktail and the lecture, then dinner. It's the same thing everywhere in all the cities of the world. Sometimes they're anxious, sometimes excited, or a bit mean. And sometimes too, there's a real friend. Always smiling, Marie, even when you sweetly tell sinister stories during your *talk*. I'm able to sell anxiety, it sparks interest, but in a friendly way. Tomorrow or the day after, we part, we embrace, we exchange offprints, books, addresses, embrace again, till later, stay in touch, OK? It's a small world, a wave of the hand, a momentary melancholia, suitcases passing through the metal detector. — Hello, are you Keiko? Thank you for coming to get me. Is Keiko too just a little stream of cultural capital? Obviously. The white-gloved chauffeur watches us in the rearview mirror, chatting politely, heads leaning back on immaculate lace coverings. The cab takes off like a rocket through the *highways* and interchanges. Streams of capital. We arrive, I get to have my half hour. The room is on the fifty-ninth floor, and everything's OK.

In the shower, Marie remembers that their prof was explaining to them that capital is not *time is money*, but also *money is time*. The good stream is the one that gets there the quickest. An excellent one gets there almost right after it's left. On radio and TV, they call it real or *live* time. But the best thing is to anticipate its arrival, its "realization" before it gets there. That's money on credit. It's time stocked up, ready to spend, before real time. You gain time, you borrow it. You have to buy a *word processor*. Unbelievable, the time you can gain with it. — But what about the act of writing? — You can write faster, page layouts, footnotes, corrections, you see? — Poor Marie, you won't get rich, you like scribbling on your piece of paper, too bad for you. You are a slow little stream. You will be passed by fast little streams. Of expeditious culture. It suffices to die before you become ridiculous. She tells herself that thought takes time and there's nothing you can do about it. Or what in general they stupidly call creation. That doesn't much resemble streams. Ponds, rather. You flounder in them. It goes nowhere, it's not happy, not communicative. Do you remember how Don works? Oh! not all shut in, like a monk! But still elsewhere completely. His friends come to see him in his country dive, he greets them politely. They tell artist stories. You can never figure out if this penetrates his brain or not. He says almost nothing about his work. And then, one day, in a gallery, there's an exhibit of his: a series of fifteen large paintings, or fifty sketches. Conclusion: the true streams are subterranean, they stream slowly beneath the ground, they make headwaters and springs. You can't know where they'll surface. And their speed is unknown. I would like to be an underground cavity full of black, cold, and still water.

Another ten minutes before Keiko comes by. Marie puts on her makeup. When it comes to gaining time, we women are always on the losing end. There's always a head and a body to replaster. Men, all they need to shine is just a little dusting. Not fair. I'm happy with my talk. They won't understand a thing. It's too laconic. And in too written a form. You'd think it was Maurice. Too "French." Or Irish. It's on the verge of being minimal. They want good, clear streams. Explain where it comes from, where it goes. A brief introduction. Situate your point in its context. Ernst maintained this, Dick objected that, Ruth explained that the problem was badly stated: phallocentric approach. And Ron, that everybody still thinks in a Western way, when there are others. Ah! others! That's all they have on their lips. Difference, alterity, multiculturalism. It's their dada.

My prof, he reminded us of Kant: think for yourself, and according to yourself. Today, they say, that's logocentric, not *politically correct*. The streams must all go in the right direction. They must converge. Why all this cultural busyness, colloquia, interviews, seminars? Just so we can be sure we're all saying the same thing. About what, then? About alterity. Unanimity on the principle that unanimity is suspect. If you are a woman, and Irish, and still presentable, and some kind of professor in Brazil, and a lesbian, and writing non-academic books, then you are a real good little stream. Cultural capital is interested in you. You are a little walking cultural market. Hurry up. But if you bring out for them a moderately intricate analysis of the *sense-able*, as Rachel calls it, and its relation to death, then you're really out of it. It's commonplace. In what way does it express your difference? Where did your alterity go? Any old guy, an honest *ordinarius* from Bochum, Germany, could do it in your place. What cultural capitalism has found is the marketplace of singularities. May we all express our singularity? Speak from your place in the sex, ethnicity, language, generation, social class, unconscious network. True universality, they say today, is singularity. Can you imagine the pretty Irish lesbian who teaches French at the University of São Paolo doing Kantian-Wittgensteinian analyses? Then, it's hopeless. It's frankly unintelligent, scandalous. So, let's see if they're like that here, in Tokyo and Kyoto.

At the agreed-upon time, Keiko comes to the room. Really very beautiful, indeed. We have a half hour before drinks. Would you like to visit the museum right across from the center where you will be speaking? There is an exhibit of Germanic drawings and engravings from the fifteenth century. Marie says that this exhibit is yet another cultural stream. A bit of the old European cultural capital, very smart, mailed to Japan, to circulate there for every useful end? What ends? Well, to show what Europe is, its past and its art, to an Asia that obviously knows nothing about it. That's good, isn't it? And you too, Marie, you're a bit of museum. And Tokyo too, and tomorrow Kyoto with a stop in Nara for about three-quarters of an hour, it's all a museum for you. Not just the promised temples, but the countrysides, the overcrowded suburbs, the urban centers, all to be archived. The destination of all the streams is the museum. They want singularities to enrich the museum.

What museum? The contemporary cultural world. Do you remember Lewis? Cultural capital, which means the capitalization of all cultures in the cultural bank. This bank is humanity's memory. Every agency must be saturated. Most of it is already done, they have saved and stored the caves of Lascaux, the tombs of the upper Nile, the Aztec pyramids, as well as the Maginot Line, and the tombs of Xi'an, Spinoza, and Agatha Christie. Now we must make archives for what is contemporary. Not only great works, but the ways of living, the means of preparing fish or arousing a woman, little dialects, slangs, the fluctuations of the dollar over medium and long durations, posters from the thirties.

They look at the Altdorfers, Cranachs, Dürers. Keiko takes notes. She is making her little archival stream, says Marie to herself, she will get there. Beautiful and serious. As if it were already done. That's what it is, the world today. Everything that is to be done is as if it were already done. Why, on feast days, do the Caduveo or Tupi-Kawahib Indians eat plates of thick, whitish larvae plucked from tree trunks? To figure in a film or anthropological manual. You see, they say, nothing is natural, everything is culture, and every culture is singular. And kinship rules? Do you think they just go without saying? Not at all. In some Australian communities, they are so complex they would drive a notary public mad. Isn't that wonderful? Put it in the archive before they croak. And the makers of simple art, do you think they're stupid? Those are the most sophisticated drawings you can imagine. Archive. And Saturn? Did you think it was a gas ball? Not so, the

sonar detected a hard center. Better redo your cosmological museum.

The next interim exhibit, Keiko tells me in her
super-correct French as we leave, will be dedicated to
the costumes, accessories, instruments, and backdrops
of the No theater in northern Honshu during the fifteenth century. And the next one after that? Dogon
masks and sculptures juxtaposed with the art of European Blacks. Say, it's rich, your museum! Keiko smiles
and gives excuses: collectors, galleries, rich sponsors.
Yes, Marie tells herself, they're paying me well too. I'm
part of the museum. No, not yet, we'll see, that's what's
playing itself out. This is just a trial. If there is a second
time, then perhaps . . . That's how they're going to listen to me. Not what I have to say, but whether I'm
worth preserving, if my stuff deserves to be committed
to memory. My stuff is not on target, that's for sure. A
little worry for Marie, and a laugh: what is not on target
might well be what is most on target. They're expecting
me to talk about minorities, I'm giving them the ana-
lytic of the sensible body in general: that might seem
singular too. The museum has to be renovated from
time to time. The streams that arrive there demand the
right to be preserved and exhibited. They must merit it,
though. That is, they must create lots of entries and
have lots of reviews written about them. What if it were
always the same topics?: boredom, a drop in the number of visitors, a counter-performance.

Marie tells herself, raising her glass along with the
center's staff, that deep down those managers are good
only if they keep making innovations. Museums, cul-

tural institutions are not only repositories, they are also laboratories. They are truly banks. The deposits must be put to work. Pieces are brought out, displayed, put back in the cellar, compared, others found, analyzed, restored, x-rayed. The same for texts or musical scores. It'll be the same for me, if I'm lucky with my *sense-able*. That's what notoriety is, an agitation surrounding a name.

Marie lays out her papers below the podium's small lamp and begins to speak, standing up in front of an audience she doesn't see. Only serving her text. She has been told that it's vulgar and unseemly to put herself forward. She has confidence in her text. It is necessary that it speak all by itself. She absents herself. It will find its own tone. As for me, this is the time when I can think about other things, that's much better. This story about streams of culture and capital is a strange business. It's metaphysical. Not just metaphorical. Metaphysics is metaphors that have been realized. Hey, this seems to interest Keiko, in the front row, my *aisthesis*. Is there a good turnout? No time to see. In any case, I am their other, that's the advantage of being exported. There are only a few who know whether my merchandise is truly singular (?). If the room is full, they will say that it was good, no matter what. If not, the public will have been deceived, and the center discredited. A strange metaphysics. Bah, it's the metaphysics of capital, flat out. Thermal machines, hot pole, cold pole, work. They fabricate what is differentiated. The whole question comes down to whether new energy is always available. And manageable. But as for managing, they have become shrewd. Their multiculturalism, minorities, singularities had no future in the culture industry a hundred years ago. Except as the Colonial Exhibit. This obligates many strategies of capture and exploitation. Finally, it became profitable. People get bored, they have enough of snacking always on the same images, the same ideas at the cultural fast-food outlets, they need a little something *live* and unexpected. A good loophole. But something else must be found in ten years. A strange metaphysics.

Not that it's new. It's dynamics as world system, which goes back at least as far as Aristotle, but what's strange, Marie thinks, is that nobody, except for a few crazy megalomaniacs, is interested in the theory of forces. It's only interesting as spectacle. That's what the interest of dynamics is, not force or power, but the aesthetic pleasure they procure. A human community who contemplates its differences. A generalized aesthetics. The great operation of our fin de siècle, of the turn of the century perhaps. Hey! Maybe they hear this in my presentation. If so, then I'm saved. They want only one thing, that one talk about them, that one show how interesting they are. Everything must speak about them. Do you remember that astronaut who said that you understand the earth and humanity a hundred times better when you see them from spaceships and probes? Halley's Comet, you remember, was met by a probe after who knows how many years in transit. It speaks about them. A humanity viewing the spectacle of itself in every theater. The repertoire must be changed. New plays found. The old ones shown differently. All this dynamics to end up *ad panem et circenses.*

The lights go on, applause. Enough? It's OK. We move on to the question and answer game. That part of the cultural. They have a right to speak, a duty to intervene, no passivity, animation, interaction. The test of a good performance. Marie, now is not the time to show that you could care less and that you've had enough. Never tired, not really? Otherwise, they won't invite you back. Have I been "other" enough? At the very least, their dialogue serves this purpose, of knowing that. Answer politely, explain, mark your alterity, don't let yourself be brought back to what is well known, defend your difference. Go on, show that your own little stream is like no other. Very animated, huh? Every question is "very interesting, but nevertheless I would like to add that . . ." And not too long, OK? There's still dinner.

We dine with the *happy few,* speaking French and English, or else Keiko translates. The streams in the capital of language need translation in order to be operational. Painting, music, they work without transformation. The questions and answers are continued over dinner. Words are swallowed along with the food, in bulk. But watch out, my dear, your table companions are the decision makers, the journalists. Too bad for the time zones. Cultural capitalism does not concern itself with drowsiness. But time differences, yeah, that's important. As they are for capitalism, period: closing time in Tokyo, opening time on Wall Street. Your little *talk* is an index of the tendency in Paris at that hour. — How do like Tokyo? First time? Full of surprises, wonderful, but you know I haven't got much time. Are you going to stay a little? Alas! tomorrow morning I have a seminar at the university and then I take the *shinkansen* for Kyoto. And Europe?

Ouch! It's hard, all this. It would be a whole presentation, even a seminar for a month or two. You're suggesting this to them? No, the request comes from them, not you. You know, I travel a lot, and then I'm just a girl from Paris, having a hard time losing my innocence. — Go on, go on! — Europe as marketplace, you know everything about that, more than I do. But Europe as culture, that exists and doesn't exist. It's like a family. — There you go. What are the limits of a family? You're not done when you get to great-aunts and nephews twice removed. Are the Transcaucasians Europeans? And the partitioning of the patrimony! For twenty-five centuries, not one border has stayed the same in Europe. Jealousies, ravishings, rapes, kept mistresses, arranged marriages, incest, the hegemony of one branch of a family over the others. Everyone adores and hates everyone else. It's not over yet, you know. Peace within the family has nonetheless been decided upon. But all the ulterior thoughts remain there. And culturally, what do you think? It's a monster. Thirty different languages, all the possible religions that have emanated from the three Revelations, along with all the conflicts that go with confessional and linguistic cohabitation and proximity. Without mentioning ethnic groupings, which do not necessarily correspond to those of language. For multiculturalism, Europe is unbeatable. Within the family, there are only foreigners. The only real community is that of interest, that is to say, that of capitalism, development. And even that is not simple. The invasion of wealthy Europe by the wretched that have been fabricated by fifty or more years of Stalinism. Unequal development, in the very heart of Europe. The new arrivals from Poland, Turkey, or Hungary parked in the Brandenburg Square mobbed by young unemployed workers, inevitably xenophobic, as recounted by Hans Peter. And while this is going on, German capital sells off the old East German enterprises and casts an envious eye upon the market in Ukraine and in Russia. The war goes on, not by arms, but by cash. So, culture, in this disorder?

Good, they're no longer listening to me, fortunately. They're making comparisons with their own situation, Japanese capital in Korea, and throughout Southeast Asia. And what will China do, in the end? That's it, cultural streams, after all. It happens anywhere and it gets lost, in the desert. Words, incomprehensible sentences, pieces of music, images, manners that are delicious— but from afar—for exoticism. Can you ever escape the bullshit of tourism? Including yours, Marie. But we don't have enough time. It's become too much for a single human life: what there is to see, to hear, to understand. The museum is too rich, the laboratory works too fast. Go to bed! You have to begin again early tomorrow morning. Thank you and good-bye ceremonies, respects paid, taxi.

At one in the morning, the hotel foyer is full of

businessmen. They're making deals, in all the languages of the world. What the fuck are you doing here, Marie? Is it that the little jewel of reflective thought keeps its hand in? There is still some capital interested in it, isn't there? Some collectors? For how long? We'll see soon. But you, maybe not, my old deary. Try not to smoke so much.

chapter 2

The Zone

Cities must be entered by way of the suburbs (*faubourgs*).[1] The sentence that goes with the suburbs is the lament: we live nowhere, neither inside, nor outside. This lament of being orphaned was already echoed in the classical city by Villon. It has spread right into the heart of the modern metropolis. Street urchins, wayward girls, the children of the zone come to the center

---

1. To understand what follows, the traditional social geography of the European city must be kept in mind. As opposed to the affluent suburbs and impoverished inner city that typically characterize urban America, the *faubourgs* on the outskirts of a city like Paris in fact group the poor or working classes *away* from the wealth of the center. The "zone" refers to that intermediary space between "bourg" and "faubourg" created by the demolition of the city walls at the end of the nineteenth century. Officially uninhabited, the zone in fact became a kind of giant shantytown encircling central Paris until the mid-twentieth-century "sanitizing" of the zone by the paving project that constructed the automobile beltway that currently rings the inner city.—Trans.

on Sundays to sing their disjointed ditties. They recite prose poems. They upset the *ars poetica*. Their names are Baudelaire, Verlaine, Rimbaud. "You read prospectuses, catalogs, and posters that sing out loudly / Here is poetry this morning, and for prose, there are the newspapers": Apollinaire begins *Alcools* with the poem "Zone." In Greek, it means a belt, neither country nor city, but another site, one not mentioned in the registry of places.

In the 1916 preface to *Le Cornet à dés* (The Dice Box), Max Jacob draws out the two traits of the orphaned work, style and situation: "Style or will creates, that is, it separates. Situation distances . . . . You know a work has style by the fact that it gives the sensation of being closed; you know it is situated by the little shock you receive or else by the surrounding margin." The work is girded by its distance from everything, from the author, from the subject, from any sources. "The prose poem is a jewel," a little threepenny jewel, upon which Bertolt Brecht and Kurt Weill also impose the discovery of distancing. It's the stuff the hobo owns. It's stolen and steals away with its thief. It's the pride of Jean Genet's slammers and slums.

These margins of the big city are not something recent. Rome, Alexandria were also girded by suburbs of dubious distinction, where being orphaned and out of work were what was sung. After all, Jesus, whose image haunts Baudelaire, Apollinaire, and Max Jacob, is cathected by the lament of those who live in the zone, of those who count for nothing. In the West, society is not a given. It seeks itself, it seeks to compose and regulate its being together and its being in the world. It decomposes and deregulates its archaisms, slaves, peasants, craftspersons, miners, workers in old factories, and tomorrow all wage earners? Over a thousand different episodes, its gesture of making itself while undoing what it is, is constant. The features and ingredients of this metaphysical and urbanizing feast cross paths in the zone: you enter, you leave, you pass. The suburb is the permanent *après-coup* of the inquiry led by the Western soul on the subject of community and inhabitable space-time.

This inquiry or *historia* (obstinate rebeginning, initiative and destruction) is inscribed in the ways of inhabiting just as *philosophia* (edification and critique) keeps organizing and disorganizing the ways of thinking. Philosophy is not *in* the city, it is the city in the process of thinking, and the city is the agitation of thought that seeks its habitat even though it has lost it, and has lost nature.

Modern philosophy inhabits the metropolis in an equivocal fashion. Relegated to its outskirts, it also occupies its center. In a letter signed in May 1631 in Amsterdam and addressed to Guez de Balzac, Descartes boasts to this landed lord about the leisure so worthwhile to thought that comes from the anonymity of a population whose driving force is business. The great republican port shelters the philosopher within a desert where the crowd of others runs into and neutralizes itself. An excellent site and a good time to draw up the plans for a city that would be entirely deduced, for a community and a thought founded upon itself. The very same year, Jacques Lemercier thus begins to deduce the city of Richelieu in the middle of the French countryside. A little later, the philosopher of the *Discourse on Method* projects the radical urbanization of thought: just as for the big city, the "irregular" remains that the fortune of history has left to thought must be leveled, in order to rebuild upon the plane all at one time "from the beginning."

The philosophy of the city and of philosophy can be less sectarian. From Hobbes to John Rawls, it is distrustful of beginnings. It draws up the state of the *trafficking* between interests, between passions, between thoughts. It tries out some principle that allows for a good regulating of the circulations it observes, on the basis of the means given to it by tradition. But whether deduced or induced, the city is in the head of all modern philosophies. And whether conceptual or empirical, modern philosophy presents itself as the head the city needs for its amendation or refurbishing. This oscillation between critical housecleaning and metaphysical repolluting cannot be born in a village. The despair of ever being able to found existences and the resolve to give them safe haven, the nostalgia for the true and the weariness of taking risks, the contrary desires to retire to the desert of scholarship and to engage in struggles, all these passages map out the indistinct zone where the urban philosopher undergoes and thinks through the challenge of a never finished installation, that of the West.

The megalopolis of today and tomorrow at first seems only to extend the metropolises beyond their limits, to add a new belt of residential outskirts to the zone of the suburbs, and thus to aggravate fatigue, uncertainty, and insecurity. But below this mere extension there are glimmers of a philosophy of being-in-the-world wholly other than the metaphysics of metropolises.

If the *Urbs* becomes the *Orbs* and if the zone becomes a whole city, then the megalopolis has no outside. And consequently, no inside. Nature is under cosmological, geological, meteorological, touristic, and ecological control. Under control or in reserve, reserved. You no longer *enter* into the megalopolis. It is no longer a city that needs to be rebegun. The former "outside," provinces, Africa, Asia, are part of it, mixed in with indigenous Westerners in a variety of ways. Everything is foreign, and nothing is.

The beautiful metaphysical edifices, in the heart of the old cities and haughty downtowns, are preserved in museum pieces. Beyond the modern suburbs, the new "residential zones" (a perfect oxymoron, if it is true that one cannot reside in the zone) infiltrate fields, woods, and rolling hills. These are phantom regions, inhabited and deserted. They wind their tentacles from one vicinity to the next. They form an interstitial tissue among former urban organs. This process is called conurbanization. It encysts the old outskirts around the historic centers.

The last bolt in the wild propagation of the megalopolis will be sprung loose when one's "real" presence at work becomes superfluous. The body as producer is already an archaism, as are the time clock and the means of transportation. Telecommunication and teleproduction have no need of well-built cities. The megalopolis girds the planet from Singapore to Los Angeles to Milan. Wholly a zone between nothing and nothing, it is separate from lived durations and distances. And every habitat becomes a habitation where life consists in sending and receiving messages.

I paint this picture with broad strokes because it is trivial and easily recognizable. With the megalopolis, what the West realizes and diffuses is its nihilism. It is called development. The question it asks of the philosopher is: what remains that is worthwhile when the presentation of every object is stamped with the unreality of its passage? There remains the way of presenting. The difference between nature and art falls apart: for lack of nature, everything is art or artifice. Development is an abstract idea, a ruler's word, that rules nothing, except decimal points. As for existence, the megalopolis views itself aesthetically. The monster of conurbanization encounters postmodern philosophy at the point of a generalized aesthetics. And it's on this point that they are found lacking.

I began with Max Jacob because he is one of the most rigorous signs that nihilism, the one from the zone, has made in literature. His "style," which is that of Braque and Picasso, shifts object and body through their various views and profiles. His "situation" impugns author, motif, public, and forms. The absolute he wants is the nothingness of relation. The Romanticist principle of "life," and what persists of it in Symbolism, is rejected.

Is there, then, a single Western philosopher before

Adorno who can bring thought up to the nihilistic level of this writing and this art? Spengler and Nietzsche are cited. But the former is but the aborted child of the latter, argued in a flat-footed way. As for Nietzsche, whose thought more or less transcribed has in effect nourished the desperate hope of the henceforth completely orphaned writers, painters, and musicians, he did not succeed in removing the pathos from the "nothing is worth anything." Writing in the form of dithyrambs and fragments does not interrupt, rather it reinforces the filiation with Romanticism and Symbolism. Zarathoustra's poetic prose, like the late Heidegger's sibylline writing, is well made for speaking the expected arrival of a "last god." It is still prophesying, just as it is said that the pre-Socratics prophesied in their time; even though the circumstances are propitious, in the artificial light of the megalopolis, for a laconism without pathos. Wittgenstein, Gertrude Stein, Joyce, or Duchamp seem like better "philosophical" minds than Nietzsche or Heidegger—by better, I mean more apt to take into consideration the exitless nothingness the West gives birth to in the first quarter of the twentieth century; and by "philosophical," I mean, if it is true that philosophizing is an affair of "style," what Paul Valéry concludes, in his very French classical way, in *Leonardo and Philosophy*.

An affair of style, I do believe this is what agitates and threatens philosophy today, which is both tempted by and suspicious of it. In the city center and in the outskirts, philosophy has been the intelligence behind the Western questioning about being in the world and being together. Philosophy asked what dwelling is, while the city multiplied the attempts at answering this question, made and unmade its layout, came and went between its history and its concept, redid the tracing of the edge between inside and outside. Similarly, philosophy built and demolished systems, worked to make foundations, reasoned through endemic nihilism, unpacked it and hid it.

But at present, the city's limits are overcome by megalopolis. Which does not have an exterior and an interior, being both one and the other together, like a zone. In the same way, metaphysics, which was urbanization through concepts of something exterior to thought, appears to lose its motive when that outside, nature, reality, God, man, is dissolved through the effects of criticism. The negation at work within question and argument turns back on itself. Nihilism cannot remain an object for thought or a theme, it affects the dialectical mode that was the nerve of philosophical discourse. Nothingness requires its inscription by thought not as a product of its critical argument but as a style of its reflexive writing.

This debt of style cannot be discharged by the philosopher simply by way of "doing something aesthetic." When, over two centuries ago, aesthetics was introduced into philosophy as one of its disciplines, from that moment on it signaled the decline of the argument's dominion (the *Urbs* and the *Orbs* of discourse). It relativized method, *modus logicus*, by situating it in opposition to manner, *modus aestheticus*, as Kant said. Despite or because of the subtle twisting of the categories by the latter in his effort to grasp the aesthetic fact, nothing can impede method from the promise of becoming a particular case of manner. Speculative Romanticism (if I can be allowed this shorthand) once again builds a system of nature founded upon manner, but it is of the essence of manner that it ignores foundations, systems, and nature.

The thought of the philosopher appears in sum to undergo a mutation analogous to the one that affects the existence of human beings in the megalopolis. You might say that the two movements belong to the same process of generalized aesthetics. The hypothesis is tempting. Philosophy would find a sedative in it: in the dereliction that strikes it, it would only share in the trials undergone by the community within a megalopolis at loose ends. Nonetheless, this consoling diagnosis must be criticized, and we must confront our despair.

Aesthetics must first be separated into the cultural and the artistic. This split is part of its very principle, as is the split between the historic-empirical and the transcendental. But it is also observable in the facts.

Culture has been a means in a strategy. First, to wage war against despots and priests, and later against the class enemy. The consciousness of the oppressed is seduced by the values of the enemy. It becomes free by cultivating itself. The combatant must be liberated in his/her thought in order to be liberated in reality. This is the vicious circle of every pedagogical and revolutionary project. What allows the child to break out of this circle is growing up, assimilating culture, and forgetting it in the process of realizing it. But it is administered too late to the old children that are the exploited—too late and too soon. They can no longer realize it, though they can still believe in it. Pedagogy is quickly transformed into propaganda.

Such is the fate of the political culture of German social democracy at the turn of the century. The cause seems to be a good one: a stepchild of the *aufklärer* project, it aims to institute communities of enlightened citizens and conscious workers within the suburbs. But these institutions are caught up in the great crisis, in the Great War and in Nazism. This is a sign that democracy has not been assimilated. When nihilism unleashes its violence, the masses lose their head. The lost head is called the unconscious. Nazi cultural politics targets the unconscious, in order to tap its energy. The point is to inculcate into this people in distress the fable of its originary destiny, that of saving Europe from nihilist decadence. What is at stake in "culture" as politics and propaganda is precisely to favor the acting out of that paranoid phantasm. Cultural politics becomes what is essential in politics. The community is "reconstituted" by climbing onto the stage where heroic figures are offered for its wild transference. Nihilism is combated only by its interiorization as a fabulous aesthetic. Political art is "culture," and "culture" is the art of directing the transference. Deployed into "living" architectures, the masses watch themselves mime the triumph of a will to archaic power.

This perversion was not circumstantial. It did not disappear with the defeat of Nazism. No doubt, the "content" of culture changes; after the Second World

War, the figures charged with the task of mobilizing unconscious energies are of another nature. These figures
are addressed to the individual lodged in the megalopolis and no longer to the citizen, the laborer, or the man
of the people, that is, to an inhabitant of metropolises.
Culture manipulates the desire for development (including that of culture) rather than that of justice,
equality, or destiny. And the media offer immense possibilities of aestheticization to the cultural politics of triumphant liberal capitalism. This a commonplace today,
and I abbreviate accordingly. One need only note that
the multiplicity of competing figures proposed by the
cultural institution of the megalopolis is essential to this
politics. It assures its permissibility and gives it an air
of critique thanks to the comparison possible between
"good objects." This plural aestheticization tends to
turn our culture into a museum.

Objects, or contents, become indifferent. The only
question is whether they are "interesting." How can
something that is indifferent be interesting? When the
object loses its object value, what keeps some value is
the "way" in which it is presented. "Style" becomes
value. "Style" is where transference takes place. Aesthetics is the answer the megalopolis gives to the anxiety
born for lack of an object. As the cultural institution
proper to the megalopolis, the museum is a kind of
zone. All cultures are suspended between their there
and our here, which is itself the there of their lost here.

But this museum aesthetics must remain under the
rule of the imaginary. It must be "interesting," that is,
offer manners, indeed, styles, rather than objects, to

which nonetheless the demand for security or protection (against the anxiety of dereliction) can be attached as if they were objects. No matter how diverse, however, every manner permitted or suspended in the museum remains under the same rule as that of cult objects: they must be "good" or "bad," giving (themselves to) love or hate. The rule of supply and demand in the libidinal marketplace.

Now, this is not at all the aesthetics with which philosophy today is faced. I shall not describe the innumerable signs, or inroads, apparent in every philosophical discipline and through which this new course imposes itself on thought. I shall only say this one thing, which directly bears on my point: the various modernisms have all been humanisms, religions of Man. The latter was for a while the last "object" spared by nihilism. It soon became clear, however, that this object had in its turn to be destroyed. The final consignment of humanism is: Man is Man only by what exceeds him.

The enigma of this excess is undoubtedly what has always intrigued philosophy. But within the aesthetic frame imposed on it by contemporary nihilism, this enigma must be thought of as the "presence" through which the absolute (which is what has no relation) makes its sign in forms (which are relation). That is, for example, style and situation in the sense given these terms by Max Jacob, as we said at the beginning. Something utterly other than an aesthetics of imaginary demand is involved here. What is involved is what the Ancients, at the time of the famous and decisive Quarrel, defended against the Moderns over two hundred years ago—what they defended and elaborated in the name of what the *Treatise* of Longinus called the sublime.

There is no sublime object. And if there is a demand for the sublime, or the absolute, in the aesthetic field, it stands to be disappointed. When commerce latches on to the sublime, it converts it into the ridiculous. Nor is there some aesthetics of the sublime, since the sublime is a sentiment that draws its bitter pleasure from the nullity of the *aisthesis*. A sorrow felt before the inconsistency of every object, it is also the exultation of thought passing beyond the bounds of what may be presented. The "presence" of the absolute is the utter contrary of presentation. The sign it makes escapes semiotics as it does phenomenology, although it emerges as an event on the occasion of the presentation of a phenomenon that is otherwise sensible and sensed.

The sensible is always presented, here and now, within forms. But what is artistic in forms, or the *artistic*, is a gesture, a tone, a pitch, received and intended, which transcends them all while inhabiting them. The artistic is to the cultural as the real of desire is to the imaginary of demand. The absolute is the empty name (empty for the philosopher of the megalopolis) of that which exceeds every putting into form or object without being anywhere else but within them. The demand for forms or manners may metamorphose itself, like styles and cultures. But desire, because its object is the absolute, is unconditional. If the artfulness of great works can traverse the vicissitudes undergone by the cultural in the course of history, this is to the extent that the gesture of the work *signals* that desire is never fulfilled. All reduction of the artistic to cultural reality is a denial of desire.

In the aestheticizing megalopolis, philosophy is found, or rather lost, in the position of being on guard against or of having regard to the nothingness that is the absolute. A pretty ridiculous position . . . The philosopher becomes lost as an intellectual in and for the *polis*, because the latter is getting lost. The philosopher gets lost as the master of concepts and of conceptual edifices; to solve this would require enrolling in the school of science and technology. It is past the time when philosophers could dream of building a metropolis for thought, as they have been charged and accredited by the modern community in making the philosopher the professor of universality. On the contrary, the temptation to think in accordance with the community or against it, to commit oneself to or draw near a party of any kind, must be judged futile or dangerous.

Being disabused in this way is not done in the name of realism, but rather in the name of the absolute. If *phrazein*, to phrase, to make a silent sign, is the only means of signaling itself that can be attributed to the absolute, I imagine the philosopher in the megalopolis being given over to phrasophilia. This would be the philosopher's (unworldly) way of being in the world. In no way a form of retreat or ivory tower. Nor is it commitment, public manifestos or declarations—except insofar as the probity expected of any citizen requires it. Even less is this the obscure return to theologies and cults.

Rather, it would be a squint-eyed look at the visible,

divergent enough to glimpse what is not visible there. An ear deaf enough not to be seduced by the melody and harmony of forms, but fine enough to take in pitch and nuance. Impassive before the seductions of the aestheticizing megalopolis, but affected by what they conceal in displaying it: the mute lament of what the absolute lacks.

But is it true that the climate-controlled aesthetics, which is the mode of existence in the megalopolis, "displays and conceals," as I just said, the suffering over a lack of the absolute? Or else, is this suffering not the construction of a fable that philosophy needs to legitimate the role it attributes to itself?

The immense zone rustles with billions of padded messages. Even its violence, wars, revolts, riots, ecological disasters, famines, genocides, murders are broadcast as spectacles, along with the following notice: you see, this is not good, it requires new regulations, other forms of community that must be invented, this will pass. Despair is thus taken as a disorder to correct, never as the sign of an irremediable lack.

This foreclosing of desire and the lowering of all signs into the imaginary of management gives to the megalopolis its strange style, namely, that of a zone that is both precarious and comfortable. Is the truth of the megalopolis exhausted in this style? Does it leave anything behind? Has the philosopher today, or the writer or the artist, gone mad when he/she insists on lending an ear to the lack of the absolute whose muffled death rattle he/she thinks can be heard in this style? Is there misery, *this* misery, even in what is most ordinary in the megalopolis? Isn't this misery what writing, Celine's for example, must bear witness to, at the price of going to the end of its night? Isn't writing, reflexive writing in particular, the writing of the philosopher today, still what must obtain the credit of immortality by snatching it from the aseptic death that constitutes our existence as rich zone dwellers? We will never *know* what is called knowledge. The megalopolis, in any case, is perfectly well organized to ignore or forget these questions, this question. And nevertheless, the forgetting of forgetting still makes enough of a sign for writing—art, literature, and philosophy all mixed together—to insist on bearing witness to the fact that there is something left behind.

chapter 3

Paradox on the Graphic Artist

— They're terribly cornered. Very little freedom of movement. Not only under stringent constraints, but various kinds of constraints, completely heterogeneous ones. They struggle in this web like crazy people. Each in his or her own way. Each one crying out that he/she is still alive. Long live graphic artists, but what does living mean for a graphic artist? To be still alive. All these constraints put together, maybe each in particular, are mortifying.

— What constraints?

— The heavy-duty ones are obvious: to be liked, to be persuasive, and to be just. What I mean to say is that the object (so I call the product resulting from the graphic artist's labor) gives pleasure to the gaze; that the object induces a disposition in the viewer to buy into (in the double sense of going there and believing in it) the demonstration, the exhibit, the institution, etc.; that the object is faithful to the thing (institution, exhibit, etc.) it promotes, faithful both in the spirit and in the letter.

— You mean to say that by targeting the pleasure of the eyes . . .

— Of those eyes that engage thought not in knowing, but in enjoying . . .

— By targeting this pleasure, the object falls into the realm of aesthetics; by targeting belief, it derives from rhetoric. And by respecting the truth of the thing . . .

— Or by revealing it . . .

— The truth of the thing promoted, the graphic object takes on the value of testimony, it belongs to the art of proving, to inquiry, to history, to the establishment of knowledge.

— They are in fact at once artists, lawyers, witnesses, historians, and judges.

— Why judges?

— Because they interpret. They are also interpreters. What would the fidelity of the object to the thing to which it refers be, if this reference were not supported by an interpretation? There is fidelity only because infidelity is possible. What would it be to represent the thing by the object, *right down to the letter*? A simple photograph interprets its subject. The "letter" is to be deciphered and interpreted. Take the title of a film, an exhibit, an institution, a play. Let's say it is the letter of these things. It distinguishes them from other things in a general table of titles (a catalog of works, for instance) but only by a simple process of opposition. It says what the titled thing *is not*, it almost never says what it is. Now, the graphic artist must signify what it is or what he or she thinks it is, even while putting the title of the thing back onto the object. The graphic artist "deals with" the thing as red or blue, figuratively or abstractly, as a realist, a surrealist, or a conceptual artist. The graphic artist interprets the thing. The way in which he or she inscribes the title onto the object, positions it, the character and font of the letters used for this inscription, are so many interpretations. And so many judgments.

— Art is free. With all these constraints, is graphic art therefore not an art?

— First of all, art is not free. It is freedom, within constraints at every level, conscious and unconscious. But then, aesthetics is an art, the art of producing or of feeling pure (disinterested) pleasure. Rhetoric is an art of persuasion. History is an art of true recounting. And interpreting is the hermeneutic art, perhaps the most difficult of them all. Its rules are almost unknown. We know mainly the negative ones: add nothing to the thing that is interpreted, do not make it say the opposite of what it says, do not ignore previous interpretations, do not impose one interpretation as definitive. The tradition of reading the Torah has blocked some kinds of positive rules by making distinctions in the text of the Scriptures between literal, hidden, moral, and allegorical meanings.

— Do graphic artists know all this?

— There's no need to know the rules, which are not very prescriptive in any case, in order to interpret something as a graphic object. It's better to recognize what you don't know. Hence, the freedom of graphic artists, chained to their constraints. Imagine (this must happen) that a "subject" is imposed on them, a poster for a public commemoration, for example. By the variety of objects this occasion gives birth to, you can see what great latitude interpretation leaves them.

— Do you mean to say that some will emphasize persuasive force, others the aesthetic excellence of their object, and still others the veracity of their testimony?

— Not only that. Each will appeal more to a given literal, allegorical, etc. sense of the commemoration, that is, of the event the poster is supposed to recall and celebrate. Take the bicentenary of the French Revolution . . .

— I beg of you. You were saying that these were just the heavy-duty constraints, the most obvious ones. What else is there?

— One more word, before we go on. The word *intrigue.* The object made by the graphic artist must be intriguing. By being intriguing, it might satisfy all the constraints at once. What is beautiful catches the eye, stops the permanent sweeping of the field of vision by the gaze (which is what happens in ordinary sight), visual thought pauses, and this point of suspension is the mark of aesthetic pleasure. It is what is called contemplation. You wait, you linger, you wonder why, how it is that it is pleasing, say, to view the *Horatii* (by David) making their oath with the meadow of Valmy in the background. But, on the other hand, that which persuades is also surprising, or rather what surprises is in and of itself persuasive. Wow, you say, I never thought of that (representing the French Revolution this way).

You give yourself over to the object as to something that has remained unthought but that you recognize right away as if it belonged to you. Just like in a dream, or a slip of the tongue. What is more persuasive than a slip of the tongue? It is certain that it means something you were thinking about, while being unaware of it, while being unaware of *what*, while being unaware *that* you were thinking it. Perhaps there is a slip of the tongue in a good graphic design, the slip of the tongue that *you* the viewer were able to make with regard to the thing promised. "La liberté de Mande la libertheid" works on the call for Mandela's freedom just like the dream works on the remnants of the day. And in the third place, what is also, above all, intriguing is the self-evidence of a truth that bursts on the scene, its tenacious trace, something other than an opinion skillfully brought out by a well-honed argument, more like a kind of immediate or "plastic" certitude. How about an example? A man's face, a woman's face, at very close range, cut off from each other by a kind of vertical tear, staring at each other across this tear, he with an intense blue iris, she with her gaze masked by a scarf of the same blue. A poster for a play: *Les Yeux d'encre* (Eyes of Ink). The plastic truth of sexual difference: the ink of separation displaced *between* the blue gazes.

— To listen to you speak, what is intriguing always stops the flow of time.

— Because the time of graphic art is one of those more subtle constraints I had in mind. Much is said about communication with regard to graphic art. But we have more material than is needed, if by communication we mean the transmission of a message. A message gives information in the strict sense. That is, an answer or a set of answers that are specific and useful for a specific question. Now, we do "have" language: conversations, interviews, and all their spin-offs, telephones, radio, fax, computers, newspapers, handouts, the mail. I cite these haphazardly, some characterize means of support, others procedures for transmission and diffusion, some interactive, others not, etc. Never, in human societies, has there been so much talking as today. We are so happy to dispose of these means of communicating that you would think it was above all a question of making sure they're really there. The message, that is to say, the information that answers a question, is pretty much neglected. On all the supporting devices, there is an abundance of false questions, the ones everybody knows or whose answers can be guessed. We don't inform, we reassure: oh yeah, that's just what I thought. The opposite of intriguing. We're starting to get bored. We dream of being upset. We wait for an event.

— Graphic art certainly derives from communication, doesn't it? It informs about the thing it promotes, it answers questions. That's its testimonial function, after all.

— In part. But it also derives from the visual arts, its situation is more complicated. It has recourse to the components of the visible, the chromatic, the organization of a motionless two-dimensional space, drawing, tracing. It is thereby the cousin of painting, engraving, photography. You know that many pictures, engraved works, and photographs that belong to tradition may be considered as graphic art. They too informed their contemporaries by visual means. Look at the Madonnas and Child by the hundreds in the museum of Siena. Or the great tableaus of battles in the Ducal Room of the Doge's Palace. And despite all this, what interests us is less their information content than their beauty or truth. The aesthetic event that they are. The absolute evidence of a visual manner. The manner of dealing with space, depth, or light, color, or just the subject matter. The Annunciation is an old subject, but Tintoretto's angel at the School of San Rocco cracks through the Virgin's wall like a missile, while the one by Simone Martini in the Uffizi makes a quivering "declaration of love" to Mary, all against a backdrop of gold. They interpret the same "thing" by visual means. Both are faithful.

— You were talking about the time of graphic artists, now we are in the space of painters.

— You might judge it unbecoming here, but there would be no unease, to compare the graphic artists we are introducing by utilizing analogous, that is, aesthetic criteria. Criteria of light, line, color, spatial composition, etc. If there are not schools, in any case there are tendencies—which sometimes share the same graphic artists. Unable to comment on all of them, I will comment on none. But all of them share the same business of having to be intriguing, in any way they can.

— But this constraint to be intriguing is due to beauty, as you said, to the powers of unexpected emotion that lie dormant within colors, surfaces, lines. Once again, it's the artist within the graphic artist who cannot help awakening them, unleashing the inexhaustible potential of sensible events.

— That's true, but it's not everything. That temporality, given rhythm by the deliverance of the powers of the visible, is not exactly all their doing. They have to be intriguing too because they have to deal with passersby, with eyes that wander, with minds on information overload, bored, threatened by a sense of disgust with everything new, which is everywhere and the same, with thoughts that are unavailable, already occupied, preoccupied, notably with communicating, and quickly. Graphic artists have to arouse them from the comforting slumbers of generalized communication, to slow down their unfortunate speed of life, to make them lose a little time.

— But this loss is profitable, bottom line. A good movie poster fills the cinema, a good logo favors investment by capturing attention, it disposes it to exchange, to commerce, to consumption, it speeds up communication. Your loss of time is a gain, counted from a marketing standpoint. Their graphic commodity brings commodities into circulation. It promotes them. Whether it is cultural and of public or social interest, or of private use and interest is a difference forever futile once culture has become part of the market and the public is privatized. With a good graphic object, a little lost time means a lot of money is made, through commercial success or prestige, for the happy owner or the exploiter of the "thing" promoted.

— Your observation is true in general, but all too

generally. What can you not say this same thing about, when in fact culture is a market? Thirty years ago, they said that cinema was unique because it was both an art and an industry. And what about architecture? And the theater? And publishing? And exhibits and concerts and records? What you're not telling is what makes for a *good* poster, a *good* logo . . . And there is where we come across the constraint I'm talking about. Graphic art is not just good to sell things. It is always an object of circumstances, and consequently ephemeral. Of course, you can put it in archives, collect it and exhibit it—this is what we're doing here. You thus suspend certain of the finalities we have designated: persuading, testifying. You retain only pleasing, which exceeds circumstance. You turn a piece of graphic art into an artwork. But you deceive and are deceived. The graphic object is circumstantial, but *essentially* so. Inseparable from the event it promotes, thus from the location, the moment, and the public where the thing happens. Grant me that an Annunciation remains as current as the New Testament. Even the painting of a coronation or a victory remains current so long as the dynasty or the regime lasts. But a film program in some viewing room today? An exhibit (justly) labeled temporary? The freeing of a political prisoner?

— I agree that the thing is of little duration and the graphic artists must make a living from this "despite it all."

— But just as the thing testified to by the object is of little duration, so is the public of little stability— what we stupidly call the public, as if it existed. And graphic artists cannot make a living without making hypotheses about the public. This is not a civilization nor even a culture, in the anthropological sense. This is the combination, endlessly unmade and remade, of temporary sensibilities . . .

— Nonetheless, the public has some constants, language, a certain idea, be it unconscious, of its national or local traditions, it undergoes definable conditions of life, of work, of economic growth or recession. And then there is the air of the time, which does not change so fast.

— But you cannot determine the proportion of these components, nor consequently between them, which the graphic object must address in order to intrigue the said public. You are reduced to making hypotheses. Even for the French, the French Revolution is not a determinate motif that would be easy to animate or reanimate by some rhetorical turn or aesthetic gesture. For the Greeks, only a few tropes sufficed to arouse the idea of the polis in a funeral oration; and for the Japanese, a few internal or external architectural dispositions from the temple and some musical and choreographic figures for a Shinto ceremony to evoke the presence of the gods. In the society we live in today, most motifs are uncertain, many motivations are unforeseeable (especially outside the sphere of retail consumption), and the art of the graphic artist is risky. You may bore when you thought to move, you imagine yourself cynical and turn out to be authentic. There is a wager to be made on the current state of the big, black beast's sensibility.

— The big, black beast? You mean the public?

— It doesn't know what it likes or doesn't like. It doesn't exist for itself as a sensibility. It knows itself only indirectly, through situations, and these no longer have the regularity of rituals. The graphic object must constitute one of these situations. It lands in a "blank," neutral, perhaps deserted, region of the public's affective continent, and it is presumed to populate it, to draw sensation to it.

— Good graphic art would then be sensational?

— Sensation is the contrary of sensational. The latter is calculable from what we think we know about the most ordinary emotiveness. It is the trivial mode of seduction. A newspaper boss "knows" what he has to get out in six columns on the front page. But whether beautiful, persuasive, or true, graphic art does not seduce. You seduce by way of an interest, a passion that you make work. The graphic artist constrains the viewer to suspend his or her reactiveness, to dream, to interrupt his or her preoccupations. The graphic artist gives the viewer over to the freedom to feel something other than what he or she believed, to feel otherwise. The graphic artist is a street artist, a peddler. The street (European, New York, Japanese) is a figure of public daily life, a scene of encounters. In the street, encounters are not tragic. Tragedy is the encounter within the familial home. What you encounter in the street is the unexpected, what "passes by," that woman passing by. The art of modern cities, graphic art is exclusively dependent on cultural, commercial, political, utilitarian events, all placed on the same gauge, subject to the same rule of what is without rules, of the event. Graphic art grasps the daily public in its monotonous "passing by," and it gives its other measure, of possible beauty and self-evidence. It transmutes the public. It brings it to see otherwise because it interprets it, and it also brings it to interpret. That's why it *stops*.

— Popular art?

— I would like to call it popular if I knew what "people" meant today. Popular arts, in Europe and outside of it, are a discovery or invention of the Romantic nineteenth century, which, for the Western world, lasts until the years of the Great Depression. The totalitarianisms, which issued forth from it, were popular and made great use of the popular arts, that is to say, the sensibilities inscribed within local traditions, with a view to *mobilizing* people. But graphic art is not propaganda. As I said, it intrigues, thus immobilizing and causing reflection. Take a Suprematist or a Constructivist poster from the twenties by Malevich or Lissitzky, and then take some Stalinist posters (on the same subjects) from the mid-thirties. You can see how the "popular" is used by the latter, and how it is put into suspense, in every sense of the word, by the former. The dissolution or dissipation of the entity "people," as is the case in the modern city, is essential to the art of the graphic artist, whether abstract or not. The public does not mean people, but the absence of the people, the loss of shared beliefs, what they called the masses, during the intermediary period, the crisis years of the depression. Today, decades have passed since the capitalist societal mode dissolved popular communities. It is in the process of straddling nation-states, well past their prime.

— Enough of this historical panorama.

— The absence of a people is what obligates graphic artists to wager and also what leaves the field wide open for them. Graphic artists "target" an object, but the target keeps shifting. It cannot be said that they commune, or even dialogue, with "their" people. On the contrary, they are banking on an unsure, unforeseeable, perhaps impossible communication. They are the popular artists of cities without people and populations without traditions. Their addressees, all of us, are inhabited by the monotonous passion of "performances," only thinking about what is possible, about what is "feasible," as one says. They hurry along. They let go of the past if it can't be exploited. "Having experience" is a depth that makes them laugh, it's ballast to be jettisoned, better to have amnesia, so you can go faster.

— But never has there been so much experimenting!

— Yes, and the graphic artist also experiments with ways of intriguing. But experimentation is precisely not experience. To explore the future is not to inhabit the past. Graphic artists stick to the present by the occasion circumstances offer them. But also because they are exploring processes as their contemporaries do with everything. They too are launched out front, and they too, at full speed, I imagine. It is a rapid art. But it is an art, and a modern one, and as such, its aim is to surprise. You have to freeze the eye, quickly. The passerby stops, turns back, and examines the poster.

— But if the passerby only contemplates the poster

and its art, all is lost. The poster for a show does not fulfill its function if it doesn't make the passerby go to the show.

— That's why I repeat to you that graphic artists are cornered. Artists, yes, but promoters too. They have to offer their work and something other than their work: the thing. Their work is an object that must induce something other than the pleasure drawn from its beauty. It is a subordinate, "applied," art, as they say. It requires of the graphic artist the humility of a servant, perhaps even a humiliation. The graphic artist signs a contract, he or she then has (in principle) the mastery to choose the thing his or her object will promote. But the contract stipulates that the object must promote the thing. The graphic artist thus interprets, but here in the actor's sense, for the actor too is a servant. Just as for the actor, there is a paradox in the graphic artist. The more graphic artists make a void in themselves, in order to let themselves be inhabited by the thing, the more the object is faithful to the thing it promotes. This is a fidelity that is not mimetic, but inventive.

— The paradox is constant, but it is obscure.

— So constant that it must be extended. Who would say that the art of the actor (or the director) is secondary, or even second? Is there even one art form, be it held as noble, that does not conceal this paradox? Doesn't Picasso spend his time in interpreting, in this sense, in "playing," in replaying therefore, scenes, subjects, treatments, already proposed by others before him (or by him)? Look at all the variants and studies together that fill the two rooms dedicated to his *Las Meninas* at the

Picasso Museum in Barcelona. They are like a big sketch-book for a poster announcing a Velázquez exhibit.

— So, graphic art would reveal a truth about art, period?

— That's it. About contemporary art, period.

— Why contemporary?

— Because of the big, black beast. How can you be intriguing, in these cities full of intrigues? How can you stop the gaze of passersby upon the Infanta's dog, when they already know it by heart?

chapter 4

Interesting?

SHE: An assigned subject: the interesting. Does it interest you?

HE: It's just that I don't know, we'll see. The noun is a recent word in French, except in the expression "faire l'intéressant" (to be a busybody), which you will allow me to ignore. As an adjective, it does not signify what interests, but rather what could procure an interest, in a given case.

SHE: Do you mean to say that it is possible the interesting might not procure interest?

HE: Yes, it's a question of tone and opportunity. The word allows itself to be modulated adroitly, just by vocalic stress, to say now: "That does not interest me, I leave it for others," now: "I'll set that aside, I think I can do something with it, but keep it under wraps," or a feigned or forced surprise, or even polite disdain: "I wash my hands of it," or else: "Good God, but that's my whole shtick, let's not rush!" to be kept for the right mouth.

SHE: Does the meaning vary from that of having a big appetite to complete anorexia?

HE: From the flames of desire to the refusal to cathect.

SHE: So, is it a word that assumes the most contrary values? It means nothing.

HE: It is very convenient. It suspends both engagement and disengagement. It fends off at a slight distance. Always followed by ellipses. A nuance in one's voice urges it toward the yes, another toward the no. But it always says "maybe." It's a prudent word, widely used by our contemporaries, like other mushy words: "sort of," "somewhere," . . .

SHE: If your broker informs you of an interesting stock, it is nevertheless still to assure you of deriving good interest from it.

HE: Obviously. That's the word in its adjectival usage. And still with the reservation that a change of direction will not vitiate the calculation of interests. My broker cannot master the economic situation in its entirety. There is a remainder that is certain, a remainder of possibilities. By saying "interesting . . . ," one marks the margin separating probable from certain revenue. The profit may be improbable, very far off the mark, or very close to it.

SHE: Are you making it into a term in the calculation of chance?

HE: That's the usage made of it by your speculator of stocks. But it can extend far beyond that. If art critics say to themselves, "That's interesting," as they leave the opening exhibit of an unknown painter, they mean that perhaps this artist should be supported. If they say to a colleague without further ado, "interesting . . . ," their interlocutors understand that the artist will be dropped. And if they ask a colleague, "Do you think this is interesting?" it means that right now they don't like it and are probably going to trash it. Is there a calculation in occurrences?

SHE: There is some hesitation and a request for a moment of reflection. Always a lapse of time held in reserve.

HE: But reflection is just waiting to see how the work of art will begin to occupy the critic's mind. And, first of all, whether or not it will call for commentary. The critic will know he or she is interested, and what interests him or her, by starting to write on the work. Interest is recognized by the interested one consenting to an expenditure of words and sentences about the painting. It matters not whether this is laudatory or pejorative. If the work of art obtains the status of being commented on, it *will have been* interesting for the critic insofar as he or she will have granted it the labor of a text and its risks.

SHE: A woman finds a man interesting. She lets him understand it. That too is a risk she runs, that she "takes on," as we say, she exposes herself, with no guarantee of "retribution."

HE: The case seems similar, in fact. But does she deliver her declaration without any spirit of gain? How do you know? Does she know? Do you believe desire can show itself with no demand? But demand awaits retribution. As for the latter's importance and even its coming due, I would like to concede that the beauty of it all is not out in the clear, but that what is not in doubt is that some interest is in the principle of her declaration, as in the critic's commentary. I will say that the object is interesting—the painting, the gentleman—which is invested without knowing how to define the interest one expects of it. The interesting would be what is also appreciated in a poorly budgeted way.

SHE: An unsecured investment?

HE: Not unsecured, *ventured*.

SHE: It would arouse a disinterested interest?

HE: Disinterested is not the word. You laugh, but this paradox has been a classic motif in the analysis of aesthetic sentiment, at least since Kant. A disposition of the soul that has no reason to appropriate the object for itself nor even to be affected by its presence. Which on its own merits satisfies no desire for enrichment, for justification, for *jouissance*. That's why, they used to say, taste—that was the name borne by the sentiment of the beautiful—does not succeed in being argued: it obeys no conceivable finality. It is, of course, driven to be shared, but one cannot conclude it from some ratiocination. Compare this to dialectics: it is interesting in the same way as the stock market calculation, because reason and reasons are interested parties. The conclusion of an argument procures a profit to understanding. That profit dispenses a treasure trove of implications: "If p, then q," in return for which at the end it holds a well-established certitude: "Therefore r."

SHE: In sum, you're making a distinction between two kinds of interesting, one called disinterest; the other, final interest. One is loss oriented, the other profit oriented.

HE: You mean to say: the interest in art and love, and the interest in conviction and money. . . Well no! There are at least two objections to be made against that partitioning. First, you have to make some concessions in each case. Your lady gives her declaration of love, my critic his work, but the financier too buys, dispenses liquid cash, and risks it in venture capital, and the logician, for his or her sake, gives credit to "good" predicates that allow him or her to calculate the proposition to be demonstrated. Perhaps misers are the only ones whom nothing interests, since they fear all the possibilities. For the miser, no "you shall have" is commensurable with the "hold it in your hands." The interesting always arouses a motion contrary to that of *holding back*, even if the gesture of letting go is immediately repressed and if the "interesting" is proffered only by denying it with a sneer. But is there an avarice of sentiments? Not letting oneself be affected by whatever it might be, an object, a person, a situation, to the point of not even judging them interesting, be it only for a second . . . Not even refusing to take the risk of investing, but to be unaware of it.

SHE: That is called repression, denial, inhibition, etc.

HE: Or hypertrophy of the ego: one appreciates only what the ego is or has, one overestimates it, everything else is nothing.

SHE: Furthermore, you have to imagine that ego-philia as a sure investment: I, at least, I am what I am, and I can thus be cathected by myself without risk. In the same way, you think you can save time, which alters all things, and the futile instability of otherness.

HE: Extreme avarice. Not the loss of interest, as in melancholia, but its folding back and concentration in the ego. The latter is then mummified, self-identical, already brought forth in its entirety as such: a dead life, you might say. But maybe that's going too fast. Interest remains within egotism, a monstrous interest for oneself, even when it produces no benefit. Nothing is worth risking the pile of gold, but the pile also is worth everything and a worth for everything. It produces no benefit, it *is* benefit, certitude. It brings back nothing, since it is without any relation to anything. But what is without relation is the absolute. Between Narcissus and Narcissus, *interesse*, that's *esse*.

SHE: Your second objection?

HE: Wait, I'm getting to the end. Can the ego's interest in itself be so pure? It could be if the ego were able to be that pure object that is impassive to duration and its accidents, to otherness and its demands.

SHE: Yes, in truth, Harpagon and Narcissus will never stop having to defend their object against possible alterations coming from "outside."

HE: And that "outside" is not external to this object. Every object is precarious, including the ego. The possibility of loss is always included in its investment.

SHE: The latter is interesting only thus, in the old sense: between the egomaniac and his/her ego, obstacles interfere and are *of import.* They call forth the strong interest of that which impedes. They require laborious counter-investments, the expense of suspicion, of strategies extracted from the miser or the chaperon (thinking of Molière's *School for Women*) through their concerns about preserving their goods. In sum, instead of the "hold it," they are haunted by the "you shall not have it." This suffices to make the one who doesn't want to give anything to spend anyway and consume some reactive force.

HE: And so, in every case, whether money or love, we come to the conclusion that the interesting asks to be paid, be it in order not to be paid. The only alternative would be, not that some object is overinvested, but that none could be and that everything would pass for uninteresting.

SHE: Melancholia, depression?

HE: Or what the Stoics preached under the name of *adiaphora*: that there are no differences. *Interesse* also meant to differ, the interposition of some duration, which suffices to measure and compare urgencies: the most interesting is what does not wait long. Now, if you display a general indifference, everything goes along at the same rhythm, caring for Epictetes' broken leg, fulfilling one's civic or conjugal duties, speaking and being quiet, dying in war or enjoying a bucolic peace, undergoing slavery or assuming charge of an empire. None of all that is interesting by itself.

SHE: You have to confess that the Stoa is quite tempting.

HE: Not at all! In and of itself, it must be uninteresting.

SHE: Grant me that there is a secondary benefit in this impugning of benefits . . .

HE: I grant you that, and that was a second objection, which is but another formulation of the first. It has long been named by the popular sentence: whoever loses wins (*qui perd gagne*). By not differentiating anything, emperor and slave alike gain that haughty difference—of being in agreement with the order of the world as it stands. An echo of the Orient . . . In answer to the question, "What benefit do you draw from Zen training?" John Cage said: "None, you are the same and stay in the same place, but three inches higher off the ground." That's no meager benefit. By being very minimalist, say in music, to the point of non-composition and silence, you gain the maximum: not a good place, some assured profitability in affective success with an audience, some revenue of subjective satisfaction, but you gain elevation. Elevation or elation cannot be measured. In the Orient, three inches is equivalent to the Christian West's ascension to heaven.

SHE: I am reminded of Freud: there is a secondary benefit in neurosis. You are as sick as a dog, but you can put up with things in your illness that you could not bear were you . . . healthy.

HE: Fortunately, what is called health, in these suspect matters, is but a state of psychosis.

SHE: You're exaggerating.

HE: Let's say, of obsession, at least. In short, you disinterest yourself along every heading, I mean with regard to "little *o*'s" just to be interested solely by the "big O."

This determines a finality, a meta-finality. And a meta-interest, too?

SHE: You were quoting Kant. Do you remember this same reversal with regard to the sublime. It's a sentiment contrary to the interests of the understanding and of sensibility. But this *Zweckwidrigkeit*, this anti-finality, is final in relation to the destination of the soul. Not to taste the pleasures of nature and art, to feel only their nullity, is to orient oneself toward the essential: namely, that there is something unpresentable. And then, what interestedness!

HE: You know, that's perhaps what a true banker seeks. Not gains made by dint of good investments, but a complete displacement of funds and absolute gain. In the quest for wealth, the same absurd logic is found as in the quest for holiness or conquest: to give and lose everything to gain everything. Ahab in hot pursuit of Moby Dick, Alexander breaking past the Indus River, Gatsby's munificence. He who does not lose his life in this world, writes Saint John, will not gain it in the next.

SHE: You'll never have a job with that recipe. Not just in a business, but even in heaven, because it's obviously interested. When you appear before Him, God will laugh: you blew off your family and your belongings, but that was in order to seduce me. But holiness must not be a draft drawn against my goodness. God thus wants you to renounce the interest of disinterestedness. Here's a heavy question: what then is interesting for God?

HE: First of all, let me remind you that God is dead.

SHE: That changes nothing in principle.

HE: That changes the fact that it was not inconceivable for God himself to be an interested party, which his absence cannot be. The Gnostics were capable of imagining that God created the world in all its evil only so that it could be redeemed. Sin, death, horror, crime, the world invested as a loss, but reclaimed for the greater glory of the creditor, and with what profit! The big *O* playing the little *o*'s to show that He is incommensurable with them and that their sole interest is in crucifying themselves to show in turn that they are uninteresting next to the glory of the big *O* . . .

SHE: Don't you find this logic of display a bit abject?

HE: What do you mean? That the incarnation, and even the creation, are the result of some enormous egomaniacal calculation?

SHE: This is what I'm wondering: maybe our contemporaries, deprived of God, and with their prudent words "That's interesting," have become wiser than your Gnostics. They suspect that even the purest ethics may be interested. After all, virtue too makes the system work, even if it seems to be opposed to it for a while. Cato was useful to the republic. The system always needs these criticisms, objections, hindrances, litigations, and even differends: they improve its performance. Maybe that's why our contemporaries are so attached to the aesthetic moment: a sigh, the provisional suspension of the principle of efficiency.

HE: They can scarcely do better. They gain a little time. They draw a little benefit in provisionally renouncing immediate profitability. But with no guarantees.

SHE: Not for them, but almost for the system. I

grant you that we have no choice. But it's just that this moment of exemption, I mean, this gesture by which thought is subtracted from the rule of direct performativity, is also a rule for optimizing performances. The sciences and the arts need this, but politics and technologies just as much. You think you're disinterested, plunged in pure research, but the interest of the system is what requires this belief.

HE: What? That opening of the mind to objects which *are* not yet, the strength to keep a space of thought empty so that the unforeseen might emerge, do you deny that the exercise of that power is truly disinterested? Wouldn't it be interesting only because the system is interested in it?

SHE: I'm not saying "because," I'm saying "in the final reckoning."

HE: But the reckoning is never closed, you know. And those moments in which the power we are talking about is exerted are precisely what forever obliges deferring its closure.

SHE: Understood. Let's say "at term" rather than "in the final reckoning," knowing that the date of term is always pushed back. But let's also say that the fruit of those moments of emancipation has every chance of being, sooner or later, gathered back into the system. Like you, I am sure that the most bizarre cosmological fable, the paradoxes of contemporary physics or biology, the highly sophisticated paralogisms of modern logics, literary, visual, and musical inventions are the feat of this power, called "creation" by theological metaphor, and which holds sway, in the extreme cases, over

Einstein, Cézanne, Schönberg, Joyce, Gödel, Freud, Wittgenstein at the end, more or less without concern over the reception its works would receive. But, on your side, rest assured that everything inscribed and deposited in the system's great register is by that very fact archived for every useful purpose. Interesting, declares development, without knowing very well why. That may serve . . .

HE: That's it, the interesting, for you?

SHE: No, it's what's interesting for the system conforming to your own definition, what can procure an interest for it, with no guarantee of success and with no foreseeable date of maturity. For the artist, the scholar, the engineer, the interesting is something else.

HE: What then? That hearkening for what is not? Its dependence on the call of a partner whose language it doesn't understand?

SHE: You don't know how right you are: try to speak that language. A conversation between two interlocutors speaking the same natural language (or two languages translatable into each other) and setting forth, consequently, the same presuppositions and the same implicit understandings accumulated over the course of history in this language or languages is a conversation that scarcely arrives at anything other than what each of the partners already knows, whether clearly or not. This is most frequently the role of conversation, to confirm what is well known. We all find ourselves in it.

HE: Therefore, not very interesting?

SHE: To say the least. Bergson said, conversation is

conservation. The same goes for the majority of interviews, discussions, dialogues, roundtables, debates, colloquia for which our world has such an appetite. They serve to assure that we are indeed "on the same wavelength" and that it's going OK. Nothing is less interesting than these repeated and rudimentary exercises in communicational pragmatics. Hurrahs and applause are incorporated into them as a priori components. What a bore!

HE: Why recall that misery? It maintains itself by endlessly consuming itself. This morning, I heard on the radio an interview with a doctor who took four and a half minutes to explain learnedly that the best thing to do, when dehydrated, is to drink water. Interesting, huh?

SHE: The only interesting thing is to try to speak the language of another that you don't understand.

HE: The enigma of translation.

SHE: If you like, but you have to extend the scope of that word, a bit too professional. We happen to grasp data (I really mean: what is already given) as if it were *also* signs made in an unknown language. For example, physical effects, cosmic phenomena, recurrent lapses, the color of a landscape, the chromaticism of a string quartet, sentences, words in our own language. Well, it might be that we grasp all that as if it "said" or meant to say something we don't know. Take for example, a caress my usual lover gives me . . . One wonders: and if that signified something utterly other? One exerts an ability of *estrangement*.

HE: That's a term from gnosis and from mysticism.

SHE: Both of them are good connoisseurs in terms of what's interesting.

HE: Come back to your "translation."

SHE: So, you make a hypothesis about that other language or other speech. And you try responses formulated according to supposed rules. Wittgenstein said: they gave you some tennis balls and, along with the balls, rules about how to play with them. And then you notice that the other doesn't use the balls as in tennis, but like chess pieces or puzzle parts or strands in a work of tapestry. These are still games known and decipherable by you. Imagine that the game played by the other is indecipherable and that the balls are used in a way that you judge to be senseless.

HE: Well, then you stop playing with that person!

SHE: Not at all. This is interesting *par excellence*. It's up to you to invent responses that accord with enigmatic messages.

HE: You don't doubt that the other is sending messages to you? That the other is not engaging in a monologue like a mere idiot?

SHE: I cannot. There is something or someone in me who is not speaking "me," my language. How can this clandestine host be ignored? You were saying that the ego, like every object, has its own alterity within it. In truth, language is what is like this. The said keeps the unsaid in reserve. What the interesting is is in rendering that unsaid sayable.

HE: Is God your other?

SHE: It's the unnameable. Cézanne comes to "speak"

Mount Sainte-Victoire in little chromatic strokes. Is the mountain done with, has it been comprehended? Not at all. Another painter sees Cézanne's oils and water-colors, and *estranges* them once again. That painter will invent another chromatic idiom. The interesting is inexhaustible.

HE: Your interesting does not have a prudent air for me, for the moment.

SHE: You said that it couldn't be. It is prudent only in the moment of suspension. But that moment pre-pares the greatest imprudence, that of attempting to speak the language of the other. If I did not expose my-self to the adventure of decipherment or of invention, the interesting would remain uninteresting.

HE: You're a lover.

SHE: Don't be vulgar. The alterity of sex is espe-cially felt, in fact, in the obstinate exhibition of *estrange-ment*, which turns love into a passion. It is felt there, it never exhausts itself. Our most total giving to each other will not prevent the fact that you are a man and I a woman, speaking two languages within the same language. Nor that each strives to decipher the other's idiom, that is, to give one another what one does not oneself have.

HE: All the while knowing that it's of no use.

SHE: Of what use is literature? I tell you the inter-esting requires disinterestedness.

HE: Maybe the benefit's discount, capitalism, what we are calling the system, is nothing but the exaspera-tion of a sordid love for the interesting: seizing upon what one doesn't have, and making it "(sur)render."

SHE: You would have to reread Marx on surplus value. It's a strange labor force, whose usage gives more value than it consumes. But only on condition that its product be inscribed within the circulation of commodities.

HE: For Marx's capitalist, the interesting is obviously the labor force. Would you say that the latter speaks a different language than that of economic calculation?

SHE: Marx surely thought that it was the other of the system. He wanted to institute it as his true subject.

HE: That didn't work.

SHE: No, the other does not institute itself as such. It can remain only interesting. It cannot properly "work or walk (*marcher*)" on its own, it makes the rest work by its being missing. The rest walks with a limp.

system fantasies

chapter 5

The Wall, the Gulf, the System

I wanted to take the occasion of this presentation to take stock of the present historical conjuncture. In the fifties and sixties, when I was an activist in that sort of "Institute" of critical theory and practice that was called "Socialism or Barbarism," everyone in the group had to take a turn at the perilous exercise known as a "situation analysis." You retained the events that seemed to be of primary importance for the historical context at that time, you analyzed them then and tried, on the basis of these analyses, to determine as adequately as possible a representation of the contemporary world and its development.

But the object of this difficult exercise was not only to arrive at the best possible comprehension of "reality," but also to define the actions by which we meant to direct the complex and shifting play of forces that constituted the given situation. Theoretical analysis was always closely linked with a practical project. We strove

hard to see things well, without bias, not for the pleasure of one's critical intelligence but so as to raise the
question correctly: what is to be done in this situation?
And in concrete terms, that question meant: how can
we, at our level, help those subject to exploitation and
alienation emancipate themselves? By what kind of intervention, here and now, could we achieve that goal?

I'm not recalling this old experience with "situation
analyses" out of pure nostalgia. Its memory helps me
measure how different the circumstances are today, and
how at present the expectations we may have of that
practice have changed. It is clear that we are not an Institute of practical criticism and consequently are not
required to draw out the lines of a political orientation.
The interventions we propose to make are reduced to
the level of publishing articles and volumes. That's not
to say that this sort of action is minor; it is other. And
the difference derives not from the name of the critical
group we form, but results from a change that has affected the historical situation itself and, by the same
stroke, the nature of criticism.

To speak quickly, let's say that the practice of activism, in our countries at least, has become a defensive
practice. We must constantly reaffirm the rights of minorities, women, children, gays, the South, the Third
World, the poor, the rights of citizenship, the right to
culture and education, the rights of animals and the
environment, and I'll skip over the rest. We must sign
petitions, write texts, organize conferences, stand on
committees, take part in electoral consultations, publish
books. In so doing, we assume the responsibilities nor-

mally attached to the status of being an intellectual. "Normally," insofar as these practices are authorized and even encouraged by legislation or, at least, by the formal and informal rules that regulate that status. Society permits us, requires us to act accordingly: because it needs us to contribute, in that order that is our own, to the development of the global system.

In this way, we can keep alive the feeling that our struggle for emancipation is being pursued. And that's not false. There is nonetheless one sign that the fight has changed in nature, which is the diminishing of the price it costs us, by which I mean the expenditure in the amount of time and energy that we must dedicate to critical practice. This reduction overtly indicates that our strategy has switched from offense to defense. According to Clausewitz, the quantity of time and energy employed in attacking is some seven times greater than that needed by the defense. Under current conditions, the war for emancipation costs us, in force, eighty percent less than before, with undoubtedly the same effect . . .

In truth, the result is not identical. Emancipation is no longer situated as an alternative to reality, as an ideal to be conquered despite reality and to be imposed from the outside. Rather, it is one of the objectives the system seeks to attain in one or another of the sectors that make it up: work, taxes, marketplace, family, sex, "race," school, culture, communication. It does not succeed everywhere, it comes up against various forms of resistance, internal and external. But the very obstacles that are opposed to it push the system to become more complex and more open, to promote new enterprises.

Emancipation becomes tangible. The system's real mode of functioning henceforth entails programs that are not just directed toward optimizing what exists but are also *venture programs*, research efforts just "to see," which generate more complexity and make room for more "flexible" institutions.

This is a very idyllic portrait, I know, and one you can find repeated to the point of saturation in political discourse, commercial messages, and administrative reports. The task of criticism is precisely to pinpoint and denounce every failure of the system with regard to emancipation. But what is remarkable is that the presupposition behind this task is that emancipation is from now on the charge of the system itself, and critiques of whatever nature they may be are demanded by the system in order to carry out this charge more efficiently. I would say that criticism thus contributes to transforming differends, if any still remain, into litigations.

From this situation, observers and commentators could draw the conclusion that the great narrative of the Enlightenment has finally won out over those representations of Man and history that have tried to obtain, over and against it, the theoretical and practical direction of human affairs. The twentieth century has still seen various types of regimes attempt to impose wholly other modes of community organization: fascism, nazism, communism. These have been eliminated from the competition. The oldest and most "comprehensive" of the great Western narratives, Christianity, has long since ceased to model real forms of social, political, economic, and cultural life. Marxism, the last offspring issuing from Christianity and the Enlightenment, seems to have lost all of its critical potency. It has collapsed with the fall of the Berlin Wall. The East German crowd that invades the stores of West Berlin bears the proof that the ideals of freedom, or at least of the free market, already haunt every head in the ex-Soviet world.

The practical critique of communism is a done deal. But what, *quid*, of the critical power of Marxism, in theory and in practice? Finding myself in East Berlin in June and December of 1989, I had occasion to note how East German intellectuals (more or less compromised, inevitably, along with the bureaucracy) were concerned about safeguarding or, rather, about elaborating a position that could have rendered us capable, us and them, of pursuing the critique of Western liberalism along with that of Eastern totalitarianism. For a mind formed by the tradition of radical Marxism, this demand rang like a call to recommence the labor that had been ours back in the fifties and sixties—that of conducting together the critical analysis of "late capitalism" and of supposedly "communist" society. The project is certainly very moving but perfectly vain.

It's always easy, of course, to understand the situation of Western and "Eastern" (in fact, broadly speaking, Central) Europe on the basis of the ascendancy of capitalism and the decline of post-Stalinist organizations and bureaucratic regimes. But one character is necessarily missing from the picture, a figure that has cast its shadow or tragic light upon the stage of history

for over a century: the proletariat. In its rigorous Marxist acceptation, the proletariat ought not to be confused
with the working class. A class was a social entity more
or less recognizable by sociological or cultural criteria;
its concept arose from anthropology, while what was
designated under the name of proletariat was the Idea
of the true project of modern history. This subject had
labor force as its sole property: as the object of exploitation for capital, it was, according to Marxism, the real
engine behind all of human history. Capital deprived
the proletariat of the use of this force in order to attribute to itself the fruits of its strange power: creating
more value than it consumes. An eminent case of "good
productivity" . . .

Marxism's stake was that of turning the various
working classes into an emancipated proletariat: to form,
out of the multiple communities of laborers caught in
the chains of capitalist relations, a single collective subject, conscious and autonomous, capable of emancipat-
ing all of humanity from the wrong that had been done
through the proletariat to humanity. There was something tragic in this vision: a society prey to *mania*,
haunted by a specter, doomed to a terrifying *catharsis*.
For the crime suffered by it did not constitute damages
reparable by means of a litigation brought before a tribunal, it was a tort, and there was no court that could
equitably hear both parties: labor and capital. Workers'
rights were de facto the rights of humanity to govern
itself. What was really at stake in class struggle was the
following right: "class against class," without regard for
nation, gender, "race," or religion.

Recalling these general lines of Marxist critique that everybody knows, one gets a feeling of tedium and old things. My way of evoking them is partially responsible for this, but the real reason is that the specter has vanished and in disappearing has carried off the last great critical narrative far away from the stage of history. The regimes that proposed themselves to the representatives of the old hero could do no more than indulge in bloody buffooneries carried out in its name. One after the other, they succumb, leaving besides their own cadavers an empty place for the reconstruction of communities on the Western model. An operation that will take years and will not pass, it is to be feared, without violent convulsions. But one sees nothing that can resist it. In this unexpected process of utterly "practical" critique, the working classes as such don't play and will not play any role. The international workers' movement has dissipated into local institutions that have no aim other than that of defending the interests of this or that category of laborers. Class struggles are elements, among others, that put up a resistance to the development of the system. But, as I said, the latter has need of such obstacles to improve its performance.

It could be said, therefore, that the "bourgeois" discourse of emancipation and the type of community organization linked to it in the age of "late capitalism"— I purposely use the canonical Marxist designations—have come out the winners after a two-hundred-year struggle. It is in vain that the other ways of reading and making history have tried to impose themselves. The system seems to have good reasons for presenting itself as the sole defender of rights and liberties, including the rights of criticism. How can the request for a radical critique, such as formulated by our East German colleagues, be satisfied if it is true that criticism, questioning, and imagination require, as Castoriadis and Lefort have shown, an open social and mental space—and that the system alone is what guarantees that opening, because it needs it?

The fall of the Berlin Wall is an event overladen with signification and heavy with historical consequences. It also has, as we've seen, decisive implications for the status of criticism. The Persian Gulf crisis, which at the time I'm writing this is still in a phase of *suspense* (October 1990), is no less significant, but in a different way. This is not the first time, and it is certainly not the last time, that the Western system as a whole finds itself confronted by the direct and indirect effects of its imperialist politics. It is clear that the Iraqi dictatorship results from the situation created in the Near East, over the last two centuries, by the presence of the Western powers. They divided up this part of the world in terms of their respective interests and the power relations that linked them and still link them together, at the same time that through this politics of partition they sought to "resolve" their inner contradictions, notably during the long crisis that gave rise to the First and Second World Wars. Saddam Hussein is a product of Western departments of state and big companies, just as Hitler, Mussolini, and Franco were born of the "peace" imposed on their countries by the victors of the Great War. Saddam is such a product in an even more flagrant and cynical way. But the Iraqi dictatorship proceeds, as do the others, from the transfer of aporias in the capitalist system to vanquished, less developed, or simply less resistant countries.

Among the differences between the regime of Saddam Hussein and those others mentioned, I will indicate two, which especially concern my topic. The first resides in the fact that the challenge Iraq is making to the Western system comes at a moment when the latter's extension has reached unprecedented proportions (notably from the fact of the communist countries' "capitulation"). In this regard, Saddam Hussein seems not to have taken the full measure of the overturning of the world chessboard symbolized by the fall of the Berlin Wall. On the contrary, the crisis that struck Italy and Germany between the two wars had no less of an effect on America and the rest of Europe.

The second difference is less circumstantial, and I will linger a bit more over it, since it is linked to the general orientation of these reflections. What makes the above-mentioned dictatorships possible is above all the distress that befalls social and economic life, no need to recall this. This distress is humiliating, it provokes resentment, and these are affective dispositions about which most minds in the West today have hardly any representation because they have not had the experience. One is humiliated because one judges the community and culture to which one belongs to be no less eminent, far from it, than those of the master. When it is a matter of an occasional and recent defeat, the humiliation remains episodic and the resentment lets itself be overcome. This is what we expect, for example, out of an unified Germany.

But such is not the case for the Near East. For centuries the Arab peoples who live there knew one of the brightest civilizations the world has ever had. Islamic tradition conserves its memory. But these peoples also know that, for centuries, Arab Muslim culture has suffered the humiliating domination of the Western powers. Let there be no doubt, the politics of "Desert Shield" has not failed to awaken a resentment that is endemic among the population of these regions. Divided as it may be between the states fabricated by Westerners, surely it reacts and will react like the sole offspring of an ancestral community that is its own: the Islamic *Umma*. And it is ready to invest in any figure of Arab birth that can bring recognition to the name of Islam and of the Umma and that can reestablish their honor throughout the world.

Here is where Saddam Hussein's force lies, and not in his weaponry. It is not by chance that the leader of a lay Arab movement, the Baa'th party, has no hesitation in appealing to the Umma to avenge the violation of the holy sites of Islam. And here too lies the true stakes of the Gulf crisis. In the short run, there is no doubt that the dictator of Baghdad will be defeated, one way or another. Nor is there any doubt that in the near future, the map of the Near East, including Lebanon, Palestine, and Israel, will have to be revised. The real problem is for the long term: can Islam continue to oppose the completely secularized lifestyle that prevails in Western and assimilated societies with a spirituality, which is marked and consecrated in every detail of daily life, and which makes Islam more the name for a total civilization than a particular religious belief? What I mean is a way for humans to be together, to which the Western way is completely foreign. Like the voice heard long ago by Abraham and Mohammed, the voice of the muezzin echoes through the cities and the deserts to remind all that there is no authority in human affairs other than the Law proclaimed by that voice.

This question of authority can serve as a touchstone if you want to identify the two parties facing off in the Near East and to determine the true stakes of the conflict above the din of arms and declarations. In the modern system, and even more so in the postmodern one, authority is a matter for argument. It is never attributed, or conceded, so to speak, to an individual or a group, which may occupy the location of authority only for a limited time. That location is, in principle, empty. Authority is designated by a contract, even if it is the final word in which the Law itself speaks.

Such is the paradox of democracy, that the supreme instance, the "foundation," of decisions affecting the community is instituted by a decision of the community. And so, the transcendence or Alterity attached to the idea of the Law and of a supreme court remains immanent to the Identity of the community. The vacating of the location of authority gives a perfect example of that "blank" or emptiness that the open system reserves in its core in order to make itself capable of criticizing, correcting, and adjusting its own performance. Inasmuch as the figure of authority is assimilable to that of the father, it could be said here that the "father" is elected by and within the community of sons and daughters.

In the Islamic (or Judaic) tradition, the father elects his people, designates his representatives, his prophets, and dictates his law to them. This transcendent, unfathomable law is accessible only by the reading of letters inscribed in the Book by the first witnesses and transmitted from generation to generation. Authority is a matter of interpretation much more than of argumentation, an utterly special interpretation that adds nothing to the letters but strives only to "fill" in the blanks between them, as we see in Talmudic reading.

The idea of authority as irreducible Alterity is surely shared by Moslem and Jew alike. The real difference lies in the manner of actualizing the moral content disengaged by the reading of the Book. The Hebraic tradition had already been traversed by the Christian message when Mohammed established the law of the Koran. With the mystery of the Incarnation, that is, the sacrifice of the son of God, and the way it is read, elaborated, and spread by Paul of Tarsis, the law of obedience becomes the law of love—that's the "good news" brought by Christianity—and the spiritual community sprung from the reading of the Book can in turn be incarnated in a concrete community. This was first political (the Roman Empire) and later economic ("protestant" capitalism). The theology of the Incarnation is lacking in Islam, but the principle that the Law must be made manifest as a secular power would never be forgotten. In order to be made manifest in the world, the authority of the Book demands that the sense of Koranic verses be fixed and able to be inscribed as a rule to follow—a situation not without analogy with what took place in Christianity: politicization and dogmatism. The authority ought (and I simplify) to be attested by successes within the century, and if those successes fail to come, humiliation arrives. In the latter, authority itself, even though transcendent, is what is felt to be flouted and not the vanity of individuals nor even the pride of the community.

Now, this was the case. Confronted by the classic and modern West, Islam was defeated because the law of the Koran did not authorize Moslem states to develop themselves as capitalist economic powers, only as mercantilist ones, while Christian dogma did not prohibit legitimating the exponential growth of individual fortunes: it could even turn that into a sign of divine grace. This blocking is at the origin of the decline of the powerful medieval caliphates. There remained the possibility of holy war. But it is ill suited in a world where wars are economic conflicts waged by other means.

Out of this overly brief and ambitious description, the following negative conclusion can be drawn at least, namely, that the historical situation presently marked by the Berlin Wall and the Gulf crisis escapes both a purely liberal interpretation and a summary Marxist one. The West shamelessly proclaims that Saddam Hussein is a tyrant, denounces the hysterical fanaticism of the Arab people, and avails itself of the violation of international law in order to intervene, as if it itself hadn't been guilty of the same misdeeds not so long ago. As for

Marxist discourse, it can legitimate its critique only by turning the "masses" of the Third World, the South, or the Near East into the substitute for the industrial and postindustrial proletariat, an absurdity both theoretically and practically, and unworthy of the responsibility of thinking.

The fall of the Berlin Wall is a much less equivocal event, to the point that it may induce a general intellection of the historical situation. It obviously excludes a summary Marxist reading, but above all it shows that a system is all the more performative for being more "open"; and reciprocally, it is condemned to be eliminated by its competitors or by mere entropy if it closes in on itself (Brezhnev should have spent more time studying thermodynamics). This logic can be applied, in turn, to the real motivations behind the Gulf crisis. As respectable as Islam may be as a model of spirituality, it cannot equal the concrete performances of the West; it will have to modify its status, for instance, by becoming a religious belief and ritual practice among others, if it does not wish to disappear in time.

In the competition between systems, it certainly seems that the decisive characteristic is openness, the "free play" they maintain within their mode of functioning. This conclusion calls forth two questions. First, that of its presuppositions: the situation must be thought of in terms of useful forces, whatever the form taken by the energy, human or material. Can one not analyze the contemporary world solely in terms of the relations of forces, that is, from the point of view of dynamics? And then: why must systems engage in competition? Leibnizian metaphysics was also a theory of systems, but the monads didn't go to war for dominance. What is the necessity that sets the competitive process in motion?

For metaphysical questions, metaphysical answers? Is it necessary? The metaphysical path, we know, has no exit. At most, it makes for an object of criticism. But what makes critique possible is the empty inner space the open system reserves and protects in its core. This system has no need for metaphysical legitimation, it does need that free space. Critique is always possible and desirable under that condition. But so too, its conclusion will always be the same: that there is no conclusion, the concluding must be deferred, that the "blank" always persists within the "text," whatever the sense one gives to the word "text." The blank is the resource of critique. It is the trademark the open system stamps upon works of the mind.

But in addition to criticism, the blank also authorizes the imagination. It allows, for example, that stories be told in complete liberty. And I would love to describe the present situation in a way that had nothing of critique, that was frankly "representational," referential rather than reflective, hence naive and even puerile. Something like a tale told in the manner of Voltaire, without the same talent of course. My excuse would be that my story is adequately accredited in very serious places, among physicians, biologists, economists. In an informal fashion, of course, even a bit timid, as if this fable were the unavowable dream the postmodern world dreams about itself. A tale that, in sum, would be the great narrative that the world persists in telling itself after the great narratives have obviously failed. That's an inconsequence, of course, about which there would be much to say—were it not for the fact that, this time, the hero of the fable is no longer Man. But let's listen rather . . .

chapter 6

A Postmodern Fable

"What a Human and his/her Brain—or rather the Brain and its Human—would resemble at the moment when they leave the planet forever, before its destruction; that, the story does not tell."

So ends the fable we are about to hear.

The Sun is going to explode. The entire solar system, including the little planet Earth, will be transformed into a giant nova. Four and a half billion solar years have elapsed since the time this fable was told. The end of history has already been foreseen since that time.

Is this truly a fable? The lifetime of a star can be determined scientifically. A star is a furnace in the void that transforms elements by consuming them. Hence, a laboratory too. The furnace ends by extinguishing itself. The glare of the furnace can be analyzed and its composition defined. It can thus be stated when the furnace will extinguish itself. So it is with that star called the

Sun. The narrative of the end of the Earth is not in itself fictional, it's really rather realistic.

What the final words of this story cause us to ponder is not that the Earth will disappear with the Sun, but that something ought to escape the conflagration of the system and its ashes. And it's also that the fable hesitates to name the thing that ought to survive: is it the Human and his/her Brain, or the Brain and its Human? And, finally, how are we to understand the "*ought* to escape"? Is it a need, an obligation, an eventuality?

This uncertainty is no less realistic than the prediction of its coming to pass.

You can see the immense work yard the Earth will be for millennia prior to the Sun's death. Humanity, whatever might still be calling itself Humanity at that time, is meticulously preparing spaceships for the exodus. It has launched an entire hinterland of satellite stations to serve as relay points. It aims missiles. Over thousands of centuries, it draws up embarkation operations.

You can see the antlike busyness with some realism because some of the means are already realizable at the time the fable is told. There remain, there only remain, a few billion solar years to realize the other means. And, in particular, to make it so that what are today called human beings are capable of realizing them. There remains much to be done, human beings *must* change a lot to get there. The fable says that they can get there (eventuality), that they are urged on to do it (need), that doing it is in their interest (obligation). But the fable cannot say what human beings will have become then.

Here, at present, is what the fable said:

"In the immensity of the cosmos, it happened that the energy distributed by chance into particles regrouped here and there into bodies. These bodies constituted isolated systems, galaxies, stars. They disposed of a finite quantity of energy. They used this energy to maintain themselves as stable systems. They never ceased transforming the particles of which they were made, thereby freeing new particles, especially photons and heat. But deprived of assignable energy, these systems were doomed to disappear in time. Energy came to be lacking. Distributed in them in a differential way to permit the work of transformation and the survival of the whole, the energy disorganized, returned to its most probable state, chaos, and spread out haphazardly into space. This process had already been identified for a long time under the name of entropy.

"In a minute part of the cosmic immensity, there was a minute galactic system named the Milky Way. And in the midst of the billions of stars that made it up, there was one star, called the Sun. Like all the closed systems, the Sun emitted heat, light, and radiation in the direction of the planets, over which it exerted its gravitational attraction. And as for all the closed systems, the life expectancy of the Sun was limited by entropy. At the time the fable was told, the Sun had more or less reached the midpoint of its life. It still had four and a half billion years before it would disappear.

"Among the planets, there was the Earth. And something unexpected took place on the surface of the Earth. Thanks to the fortuitous conjugation of various forms of energy—the molecules making up the elements of the Earth, especially water, the filtering of solar radiation by the atmosphere, the fluctuating temperature— it happened that more complex and more improbable systems (cells) synthesized themselves out of molecular systems. This was the first event whose enigmatic occurrence would condition the rest of the story, and even the possibility of its being recounted. The formation of so-called living cells meant, in effect, that differentiated systems of a certain order, the mineral realm, could under certain conditions, such as those then existing on the Earth's surface, produce differentiated systems of a higher order, the first algae. A process contrary to entropy was therefore possible.

"An especially remarkable sign of the complexifying represented by single-celled creatures was their ability to reproduce themselves by dividing into two parts almost identical to the original but independent of it. What was called scissiparity seemed to assure the perpetuation of single-celled systems in general, despite the disappearance of individuals.

"This is how life and death were born. As opposed to molecules, living systems were obligated, in order to survive, to consume external energy in a regular fashion (metabolism). On the one hand, this dependence made them extremely fragile, since they lived under the threat of a lack of energy appropriate for their metabolism. On the other hand, through this rush of external energy, they found themselves exempt from eventually disappearing, the predictable fate of isolated systems. Their life expectancy could be 'negotiated,' at least within certain limits.

"Another event came to affect living systems: sexual reproduction. This reproductive procedure was much more improbable than scissiparity, but it allowed the offspring to differ a lot more from their progenitors, since their ontogenesis proceeded from the more or less aleatory combination of two distinct genetic codes. The margin of uncertainty widened with each succeeding generation. Unexpected events had a greater chance of being produced. In particular, a 'misreading' of the parental codes could give rise to genetic mutations.

"As for the following sequence in this story, it had already been recounted by a certain Mr. Darwin. What he called evolution was remarkable in that it supposed no finality—no more than did the preceding sequence (which had led from physics to biology)—only the principle of the mechanical selection of the best 'adapted' systems. New living systems would appear by chance. They found themselves confronted by the systems that were already existing, since all of them had to procure energy to survive. With energy sources being of a limited quantity, competition between systems was inevitable. So was born war. The most efficient systems had the best chances of being selected, mechanically.

"And so it was after some time (very brief by the standard of the astronomical clock) that the system called Humankind was selected. This was an extremely unlikely system—and exactly as unlikely as it is for a four-legged creature to stand up on the soles of its rear paws. The immediate implications of this stance are known: the hands are freed for grasping, the cranial cavity restores its balance along the vertical axis, offering a more spacious volume for the brain, the mass of cortical neurons grows and is diversified. Complex corporeal skills (*techniques*), especially manual ones, appeared at the same time as those symbolic skills we call human languages. These skills were supple and efficient prostheses that allowed the Human system, so unlikely and so precarious, to compensate for its weakness in the face of its adversaries.

"Along with these skills, something happened that was just as unexpected as what had happened with the appearance of single-celled life, which was endowed with the ability to reproduce by itself. In the same way, symbolic language, thanks to its recursiveness, had the ability to recombine its elements infinitely while still making sense, that is, giving something to think and to act upon. Symbolic language, being self-referential, had moreover the capacity to take itself as its own object, hence to provide its own memory and critique. Supported by these properties of language, material technique in turn underwent a mutation: it could refer to itself, build on itself, and improve its performance.

"Moreover, language allows humans to inflect the initially rigid (almost instinctual) forms by which they lived together in early communities. Less likely forms of organization, each one different from the others, were born. They entered into competition. As for every living system, their success depended on their aptitude to discover, capture, and safeguard the energy sources they needed. In this regard, two great events marked the history of human communities, the Neolithic revolution and the Industrial Revolution. Each discovered new energy sources and new means of exploiting them, thereby affecting the structure of the social systems.

"For a long time (if you count in human time), techniques and collective institutions appeared by chance. The survival of the unlikely and fragile systems that were human groups thus remained out of their control. So it is that it happened that the most sophisticated techniques were considered as curiosities and neglected to the point of falling into oblivion. It also happened that communities that were more differentiated than others in political or economic matters were defeated by simpler but more vigorous systems (as had been the case among living species).

"Just as the properties of symbolic language allowed material skills to be conserved, corrected, and optimized in their efficiency, so it was with the modes of social organization. The task of assuring the survival of communities required the ability to control the external or internal events that might strike a blow at their provisions of energy. Instances of authority, charged with this control, appeared in the social, economic, political, cognitive, and cultural fields.

"After a time, it happened that the systems labeled liberal democratic showed themselves to be the most appropriate at exercising these regulations. They in effect left the control programs open to debate, they in principle allowed each unity to accede to decision functions, they thereby maximized the quantity of human energy useful to the systems. This flexibility turned out in the long run to be more efficient than the rigid fixation of roles in stable hierarchies. In opposition to the closed systems that had emerged in the course of human history, liberal democracies in their very core admitted a kind of competition between the units in the system. This space favored the blossoming forth of new material, symbolic, and communitarian techniques. Of course, there thus resulted frequent crises that were sometimes dangerous for the survival of these systems. But, on the whole, the performativity of the latter found itself increased. This process was called progress. It induced an eschatological representation of the history of human systems.

"In the long run, the open systems won out completely over all the other systems (human, organic, and physical) locked in struggle on the surface of the planet Earth. Nothing appeared able to stop, or even guide, their development. Crises, wars, revolutions contributed to accelerate all this, especially by giving access to new sources of energy and by establishing new control over their exploitation. It even became necessary that the open systems temper their success over other systems in order to preserve the ensemble called an ecosystem from a catastrophic deregulation.

"Only the ineluctable disappearance of the entire solar system seemed like it ought to check the pursuit of development. In response to this challenge, the system already (at the time the fable was told) had begun to develop prostheses able to perpetuate it after the disappearance of the energy resources of solar origin that had contributed to the appearance and survival of living and, in particular, human systems.

"At the time this story was told, all research in progress was directed to this aim, that is, in a big lump: logic, econometrics and monetary theory, information theory, the physics of conductors, astrophysics and astronautics, genetic and dietetic biology and medicine, catastrophe theory, chaos theory, military strategy and ballistics, sports technology, systems theory, linguistics and potential literature. All of this research turns out, in fact, to be dedicated, closely or from afar, to testing and remodeling the so-called human body, or to replacing it, in such a way that the brain remains able to function with the aid only of the energy resources available in the cosmos. And so was prepared the final exodus of the negentropic system far from the Earth.

"What a Human and his/her Brain—or rather the Brain and its Human—would resemble at the moment when they leave the planet forever, before its destruction; that, the story does not say."

Realism is the art of making reality, of knowing reality and knowing how to make reality. The story we just heard says that this art will still develop a lot in the future. Reality will be changed; making, knowing, and know-how will be changed. Between what we are and what the hero of the final exodus shall be, reality and the art of reality will have been at least as metamorphosed as they have been from the amoebas to us. The fable is realist because it recounts the story that makes, unmakes, and remakes reality. It is also realist because it takes note of the fact that this force has already greatly transformed reality and its art, and that, except for a catastrophe, this transformation ought to be pursued. It is realist, once more, insofar as it admits an inevitable obstacle to the pursuit of this transformation, the end of the solar system. Finally, is it realist when it predicts that this obstacle shall be overcome and that the force will evade disaster?

The fable tells the story of a conflict between two processes affecting energy. One leads to the destruction of every system, of every body, living or not, that exists on planet Earth and in the solar system. Inside this continuous and necessary entropic process, another process, contingent and discontinuous, at least for a long time, acts in the opposite direction through the increasing differentiation of these systems. The latter movement cannot put the brakes on the former (unless we find a way to furnish the Sun with motor fuel), but it can elude the catastrophe by abandoning its cosmic site, the solar system.

On Earth as elsewhere, entropy leads energy toward the most likely state, a kind of corpuscular *soup*, a cold chaos. Negative entropy combines energy, on the contrary, into differentiated systems, more complex ones, or let's say, more *developed* ones. Development is not an invention made by Humans. Humans are an invention of development. The hero of the fable is not the human species, but energy. The fable narrates a series of episodes marking now the success of what is most likely, death, and now the success of what is least likely and most precarious, and what is also the most efficient, the complex. It's a tragedy about energy. Like *Oedipus Rex*, it ends badly. Like *Oedipus at Colonus*, it admits a final remission.

The hero is not a subject. The word energy says nothing, except that there is some force. What happens to energy, its formation into systems, their death or survival, the appearance of more differentiated systems, it knows nothing and does not *want* any of it. It obeys blind, local laws and chance.

The human species is not the hero of the fable. It is a complex form of organizing energy. Like the other forms, it is undoubtedly transitory. Other, more complex forms may appear that will win out over it. Perhaps one of these forms is preparing itself through techno-scientific development right from the time when the fable is being recounted. That's why the fable cannot begin to identify the system that will be the exile's hero. It can merely predict that this hero, if it succeeds in escaping the destruction of the solar system, *will have* to be more complex than the human species is at the time when the fable is being recounted, since this species does not then have the means of its exile, although it is the most complex organization of energy we know in the Universe.

It will have to be more complex since it will have to be able to survive the destruction of the terrestrial context. It will not suffice for some living organism, in symbiosis with the specific energies it may find on Earth, that is to say, the human body, to continue to feed this system and especially the brain. It will have to be able to use directly the only forms of physical energy available in the cosmos: particles that are not already organized. That's why the fable lets it be understood that the exile's hero, destined to *survive* the destruction of terrestrial life, will not be a mere survivor, since it will not be alive in the sense we understand the word.

This condition is a necessary one, but at the time the fable is being recounted, no one can say how it will be met. There is uncertainty in this story because negative entropy acts in a contingent fashion and because the appearance of more complex systems—despite research and controls that are in themselves systematic— remain unforeseeable. This appearance can be facilitated but not ordered. One of the characteristics of the open systems the fable calls "liberal democratic" is to leave open certain spaces of uncertainty that are apt to facilitate the appearance of more complex organizations, and this, in every realm. What we call research is a case, become trivial, of these spaces freed for invention and discovery. This case is itself the sign of a superior development, where necessity and chance are combined not only in the epistemological order, as Monod saw, but in the reality of a new alliance, in the terms of Prigogine and Isabelle Stengers. This alliance is not that of the objective with the subjective, but that of rule and chance, or of consecution and discontinuity.

Were there not such uncertain regions in the history of energy, the fable itself that tells this story would not be possible. For a fable is an organization of language, and language is a very complex state of energy, a symbolic technical apparatus. Now, in order to be deployed, fabulation calls for a kind of spatiotemporal and material emptiness, in which linguistic energy is not invested in the direct constraints of its exploitation as making, knowing, and know-how.

In the fable, linguistic energy is expended for imagining. It therefore does fabricate a reality, that of the story it tells, but this reality is left in suspense with regard to its cognitive and technical use. It is exploited reflexively, that is, referred back to language in order to link on to its topic (which I am in the process of doing). This putting into suspense distinguishes poetics from practice and pragmatics. Fabulation maintains this reality in reserve and *apart* from its exploitation within the system. This reality is called imaginary. The existence of imaginary realities presupposes, in the system where it appears, zones that are neutralized, so to speak, in relation to the merely realist constraints of the said system's performativity. Rigid systems like a bent bow or even an instinctual program (to borrow examples from living things we know) prohibit amoebas, sycamores, or eels from fabling, as a general rule.

Realism accepts and even requires the presence of the imaginary within it, and that the latter, far from being something foreign to reality, is one of its states, the nascent state. Science and technology themselves fable no less, and are no less poetic than painting, literature, or film. The only difference between them lies in the verification/falsification constraint of the hypothesis. The fable is a hypothesis that exempts itself from this constraint.

The fable we heard is neither recent nor original. But I claim that it is postmodern. Postmodern does not

signify recent. It signifies how writing, in the broadest
sense of thought and action, is situated after it has suc-
cumbed to the contagion of modernity and has tried to
cure itself of it. Now, modernity is not recent either. It
is not even an epoch. It is another state of writing, in
the broad sense of the word.

The first traits of modernity can be seen to appear
in the work done by Paul of Tarsis (the apostle), then
by Augustine, to make an accommodation between the
pagan classical tradition and Christian eschatology. A
distinctive element of the modern imaginary is historicity, which is absent in the ancient imaginary. The moderns subordinate the legitimation of the collective subject called Europe or the West to the deployment of
historical time. With Herodotus and Thucydides, Livy
and Tacitus, the Ancients did, of course, invent *history*
in opposition to myth and epic, the other narrative genres. And, on the other hand, with Aristotle, they elaborated the concept of *telos*, of the end as perfection, and
teleological thinking. But eschatology, properly called,
which governs the modern imaginary of historicity, is
what the Christianity rethought by Paul and Augustine
introduced into the core of Western thought. Eschatology recounts the experience of a subject affected by a
lack, and prophesies that this experience will finish at
the end of time with the remission of evil, the destruction of death, and the return to the Father's house, that
is, to the full signifier.

Christian hope tied to this eschatology is re-
grounded in the rationality issuing from pagan classi-
cism. It becomes reasonable to hope. And, reciprocally,

Greek reason is transformed. It is no longer the equitable sharing of arguments between citizens deliberating over what must be thought and done in the ordeal of tragic destiny, political disorder, or ideological confusion. Modern reason is sharing with others, whoever they may be (slaves, women, immigrants), the experience proper to each of having sinned and having been acquitted. The ethics of *virtù* crown the ancient exercise of reason; that of *pardon*, its modern exercise. Classical consciousness is in conflict with the passionate disorders that shake up Mount Olympus. Modern consciousness, in full confidence, places its fate in the hands of a single just and good father.

This characterization may appear too Christian. But over countless episodes, lay modernity maintains this temporal device, that of a "great narrative," as one says, which *promises* at the end to reconcile the subject with itself and the overcoming of its separation. Although secularized, the Enlightenment narrative, Romanticist or speculative dialectics, and the Marxist narrative deploy the same historicity as Christianity, because they conserve the eschatological principle. The completion of history, be it always pushed back, will reestablish a full and whole relation with the law of the Other (capital *O*) as this relation was in the beginning: the law of God in the Christian paradise, the law of Nature in the natural right fantasized by Rousseau, the classless society, before family, property, and state, imagined by Engels. An immemorial past is always what turns out to be promised by way of an ultimate end. It is essential for the modern imaginary to project its legitimacy forward while founding it in a lost origin. Eschatology calls for an archaeology. This circle, which is also the hermeneutical circle, characterizes *historicity* as the modern imaginary of time.

The fable we heard is a narrative, of course, but the history it recounts offers none of the principal traits of historicity.

First of all, it is a physical history, it is concerned only with energy and matter as a state of energy. Humankind is taken for a complex material system; consciousness, for an effect of language; and language, for a highly complex material system.

Then, the time that is put into play in this history is no more than diachrony. Succession is cut into clock units arbitrarily defined on the basis of supposedly uniform and regular physical movements. This time is not a temporality of consciousness that requires the past and the future, in their absence, to be nonetheless held as "present" at the same time as the present. The fable admits such a temporality only for the systems endowed with symbolic language, which in effect allow memorization and anticipation, that is, the presentifying of absence. As for the events ("it happened that . . .") that punctuate the fabulous history of energy, the latter neither awaits nor retains them.

In the third place, the end of this history is in no way directed toward the horizon of an emancipation. Of course, the end of the fable recounts the rescue of a very differentiated system, a kind of super-brain. That it can anticipate this outcome and prepare for it comes from the fact that it necessarily possesses a symbolic language of some sort, otherwise it would be less complex than our brain. The effect or the sentiment of a finality proceeds from this capacity of symbolic systems. They allow, of course, for more control of what comes to pass in the light of what has come to pass. But rather than a hermeneutic circle, the fable represents this effect as the result of a cybernetic loop regulated toward growth.

In the fourth place, for us today, the future the fable recounts in the past tense (not by chance) is not an object of hope. Hope is what belongs to a subject of history who promises him/herself—or to whom has been promised—a final perfection. The postmodern fable tells something completely different. The Human, or his/her brain, is a highly unlikely material (that is, energetic) formation. This formation is necessarily transitory since it is dependent on the conditions of terrestrial life, which are not eternal. The formation called Human or Brain will have been nothing more than an episode in the conflict between differentiation and entropy. The pursuit of greater complexity asks not for the perfecting of the Human, but its mutation or its defeat for the benefit of a better performing system. Humans are very mistaken in their presuming to be the motors of development and in confusing development with the progress of consciousness and civilization. They are its products, vehicles, and witnesses. Even the criticisms they may make of development, its inequality, its inconsistency, its fatality, its inhumanity, even these criticisms are expressions of development and contribute to it. Revolutions, wars, crises, deliberations, inventions, and discoveries are not the "work of man" but effects and conditions of complexifying. These are always ambivalent for Humans, they bring them the best and the worst.

Without going any further, it can be seen clearly enough that the fable does not present the traits of a modern "great narrative." It does not respond to the demand for remission or emancipation. For lack of an eschatology, the conjugated mechanicalness and contingency of the story it tells leave thought suffering for lack of finality. This suffering is the postmodern state of thought, what is by agreement called in these times its crisis, its malaise, or its melancholia. The fable brings no remedy for this state, it proposes an explanation for it. An explanation is neither a legitimation nor a condemnation. The fable is unaware of good and evil. As for truth and falsehood, they are determined according to what is operational or not at the time judgment is made, under the regime of what has been called realism.

The *content* of the fable gives an explanation for the crisis, the fabulous narrative is by itself an expression of the crisis. The content, the meaning of what it is talking about, signifies the end of hopes (modernity's hell). The *form* of the narrative inscribes this content onto the narrative itself, reducing it in class to that of mere fable. A fable is exposed neither to argumentation nor to falsification. It is not even a critical discourse, but merely imaginary. This is how it exploits the space of indetermination the system keeps open for hypothetical thought.

This is also how it turns itself into the almost infantile expression of the crisis of thought today: the crisis of modernity, which is the state of postmodern thought. With no cognitive or ethico-political pretension, the fable grants itself a poetic or aesthetic status. It has worth only by its faithfulness to the postmodern affection, melancholia. It recounts its motive, first of all. But by the same token, every fable is melancholic, since it supplements reality.

It could be said that the fable we heard is the most pessimistic discourse the postmodern can hold forth about itself. It merely continues the discourses of Galileo, Darwin, and Freud: man is not the center of the world, he is not the first (but the last) among creatures, he is not the master of discourse. All that's needed, in order for the fable to qualify as pessimistic, is the concept of an absolute evil, one that remains independent of the imaginaries produced by the human system.

But, after all, this fable asks not that it be believed, only that we reflect on it.

chapter 7

"The earth had no roads to begin with"

Kōyama Iwao says: "The subject (*shutai*) of moral energy should be the nation (*kokumin*). The nation is the key to every problem. Moral energy has nothing to do with individual or personal ethics, or the purity of blood. Both culturally and politically the nation is the center of moral energy."

Kōsaka Maasaki says: "That is right. The folk (*minzoku*) in itself is meaningless. When the folk gains subjectivity (*shutaisei*), it necessarily turns into a national folk (*kokka-teki minzoku*). The folk without subjectivity or self-determination (*jiko gentei*), that is, the folk that has not transformed itself into a nation *(kokumin)* is powerless. For instance, a folk like the Ainu could not gain independence, and has eventually been absorbed into other folk (that has been transformed into) a nation. I wonder if the Jews would follow the same fate. I think the Subject of World History must be a national folk in this sense."

This was in November 1941. The two philosophers of the Kyoto School were trying in these terms to legitimate the factual domination of Japan over the "Great East Asian Coprosperity Sphere." If China had been defeated, it was because it was not a "national folk." Japan knew "how to decide for itself"; it manifested itself as a subjectivity.

Three months later, while Japan was engaged in the Pacific against the West, the same interlocutors, once again brought together at a colloquium, agreed in declaring that the political stakes were henceforth in deciding, between the Occidental and the Oriental, "which morality will play a more important role in the World History in the future."[1]

I'm taking in the principal motifs of this political philosophy. Its legitimacy is due neither to ethics nor to race, but to the greater power (or energy). The greater power is the one that decides for itself (*jiko gentei*). A subject is whatever constitutes itself. A natural community, the folk is only given, issuing forth from the past and cast into history. It detains its authentic power only from being able to project its history and envisage its future. This power, which transforms the folk into a nation, requires the formation of a state. Actualized in and by its state, the true power of the "national folk" *manifests* itself: it measures itself against the power of other folk and fights it. For subjectivity cannot be shared. There is only

---

1. I take these texts from Naoki Sakai, "Modernity and Its Critique: The Problem of Universalism and Particularism," in *Postmodernism and Japan,* a special issue of *The South Atlantic Quarterly* 87, 3 (Summer 1988), pp. 475–504.

one history for the entire human world, there is only one subject for that history. As the fulfillment of the power latent in all folk, the subject is called upon to dominate not just Greater Asia, but the West as well. All the particular traditions of being-together are gathered into the subject and deliver their energy as a universal project.

The State as a moment in the self-consciousness of the folk, the oneness of world history: here, we recognize the essential motifs of the political philosophy and practice of the modern West. The idea of an emancipatory finality is also European (and thus American). Takeuchi Yoshimi insists that Japan modernizes itself only by resisting the modern West, but that, in this struggle, it must repeat the Western models. How can it accede to its subjectivity if it thus remains dependent on its adversary?[2] The recurrence of European metaphysical motifs, the oneness and finality of history, power, and will, the dialectics of inwardness and outwardness, betrays this dependence, as if politics could be thought of only in its Greco-Christian form: Greek through the concept of the State and of decision, Christian by that of teleological history.

You could maintain that Heidegger's historico-political thought followed an analogous fate. In *Being and Time*, that thought strives to extract itself from the metaphysical tradition of the historico-political elaborated within speculative idealism. It tries to "constitute,"

---

2. Takeuchi Yoshimi, "Kindai towa nanika" ("What Is Modernity?"), in *Takeuchi Yoshimi zenshû (Complete Works of Takeuchi Yoshimi)*, vol. 4 (Tokyo, 1980), p. 130; cited in Naoki Sakai, pp. 496–501. Takeuchi Yoshimi's article was written after 1945.

in the phenomenological sense, the objects of thought that are temporality, being-together, historicality, thrownness and projecting, from the existential-ontological description of *Dasein. Dasein* is not a subject, of course. It is only the enigma that there is the *there*.

In the second part of *Being and Time*, in which the questions of historicality and being-together are analyzed, Heidegger's thought follows through in its effort to keep these questions at a remove from metaphysical categories. Of course, the way of being-thrown-together toward the emergence and the anxiety of the "not-yet-being," the *Geschick*, is called *Volk*, folk, without any critique or elaboration of the usage of this term. But there is no question of the folk-*Volk* being mediated by some state formation to arrive at self-consciousness. The latter is not at all at issue. On the contrary, the folk must deepen its essence, which is that of being-thrown-together into time and anxiety and doomed to projecting and decision making, in order to accede to its authentic being. The objectifying of the folk by the mediation of consciousness and the State would signify, on the contrary, a loss of this authenticity.

Such is no longer the case in the political texts from the years 1933–34. (Added to those already catalogued is the summer seminar of 1934, published by Victor Farias, under the title *Logik*, and based on class notes gathered in the Weiss archives.[3]) The Rector of the Uni-

----

3. *Lógica. Lecciones de M. Heidegger (semestre verano 1934) en el legado de Helene Weiss* (Barcelona: Anthropos e MEC, 1991). The edition is bilingual German-Spanish.

versity of Freiburg is engaged in the powerful movement that has swept the German youth. The crisis that
has fallen on Germany for years takes on at this time
such a violence that there appears to be no way out. In
the depth of anxiety and despair that seizes young people, especially students, Heidegger recognizes something of what he described in *Being and Time* under the
rubric of *Geschick*. He places his university authority in
the service of the movement in order to preserve its authenticity. He will be its guide by helping it direct itself
toward its "resoluteness" (*Entschlossenheit*).

But now this direction must be concretely indi-
cated. It does not suffice to "describe" it as an existential-
ontological trait of being-together. Now, the NSDAP,
the Nazi party, is in power and claims to assume the
role of this direction. Whence, a double shift in Heideggerian thought: it must complete the philosophical
analysis through "operators" or pragmatic notions allowing its inscription within the political sphere as it stands
now; and as this sphere is dominated by Nazi ideology,
concessions have to be made, at least in form, to the
party's ideologemes. These, of course, are the vulgar and
eclectic expression of the principal motifs of Western
metaphysics in the matter of history and politics.

The *Rectoral Address* ("The Self-Assertion of the
German University") is a striking example of this transformation. The German folk will be saved from destruction—from "absorption," Kōsaka would have said—only
if it has the means of knowledge, work, and defense of
its being-together. Whence the motif of the three services (*Dienste*) that are the University, the workers' orga-

nization (the Corporation), and the Army. All three are institutions committed to deploying the authentic being of the folk. Together they form the popular State. Now, it is clear that this determination of the three functions does not arise from an existential-ontological analysis, but from the oldest of representations of the political community in the so-called Indo-European West, especially in Plato (Dumézil). The tripartite division of power into knowing, producing, and combating thus draws Heideggerian thought near the same ideologemes that haunt Kōyama and Kōsaka, and which are the ideologemes of Western metaphysics.

Can you act and think in politics without being captivated by these metaphysical motifs? Aren't they born with politics itself? Far away as you try to escape from them, it seems they have to return, whether you are Heidegger or Japanese (and it is known how the first could recognize something of his mode of thinking in the second), and from this instant it becomes a question of "engaging in politics." (Machiavelli, perhaps, is the exception.)

Wrongly or rightly, I imagine the figure of the Jew is not of primary importance in the explicit, or even hidden, tradition of the Japanese. This is why it is remarkable that Kōsaka thinks it is a good idea to refer to the Jews at the same time as he refers to the Ainu to buttress his argument that a folk that does not transform itself into a nation is doomed to disappear.

It is true that this disappearance is envisaged by Kōsaka only as the absorption of this folk within a national, popular entity. In December 1941, the Final Solution to the question of European Jewry, that is, its extermination, had not yet been "decided" by the Nazi authorities. But already more than a decade, almost two decades, had passed in which "the jew" had been designated by the Hitlerians as the inexpiable enemy and during which Jews had been hunted down throughout all of Central Europe. Kōsaka cannot be unaware of this. And that's why he refers to the "fate" of the jew, despite the context of his reflections, which are in appearance purely Asian.

This is because the various politics of popular power and of state decision-making are never satisfied to designate their visible adversaries in the folks and States they are fighting. You would say they have a need to invent the pestilence of an internal contamination. In truth, they do not at all invent it. In effect, they have to silence something that, below the scene on which they operate and represent their tragedies, never stops threatening that scene itself, by questioning and miming the spectacle of the political. "Jew" is the name of that which resists the principle of self-assertion, "jew" is that which laughs at the will to power and criticizes the blind narcissism of the community (including the Jewish community) haunted by the desire of its own subjectivity. Under the epithet "jew" is denounced the conviction that dependence is constitutive, that there is the Other, and that wanting to eliminate that Other in some universal project for autonomy is an error and leads to crime.

The jews got this lesson of a secret, muffled, and bending—not political—resistance to the Western metaphysics of will and self-determination from a Book. The Ainu were victims of big politics because they are a blood and a soil, and because blood and soil are part of the political scene, are elements of political tragedy. "The jews" are exiled, scattered, oppressed, and assimilated on this scene, but they don't belong to it. They belong to the Covenant with the Other that is promised and registered in the Book.

This is the resistance that has to be annihilated, that must not stop being forgotten because it has never stopped being "present" to metaphysical Europe as what it hasn't been and will not be able to say, as the impotence of its potency. This resistance simply mumbles: the Other is prior to the Self.

The Heidegger of *Being and Time*, and the Heidegger who, after the *Kehre*, the turning point, elaborates the ontological difference, comes near this resisting thought. But he transcribes it and betrays it into a knowledge, or into a saying, into a poem, when the primacy of the Other requires the prose of practical respect: you, here and now, in your banality and your anonymity, you are the face of the Other (Levinas).

Heidegger missed what he sought only by a little: that which in the modern is not modern, and in the West is not Western. But this miss permitted his close dealings with Nazism and his silence about the Shoah. Too Greek and too Christian, at least in the sense whereby Christian is compatible with pagan (by incarnation), his resistance found at its end only Being, and not the Other.

In the West, Orientalism is a way of taking hold of

Asia. In Japan, modernization is a way of taking hold of Europe and America. But these are trivial qualifications. Neither the West nor Japan is reducible to these imperialisms. Imperialism, the imperial philosophy of history and politics, is Western and Japanese on the same level and in its depths, because annulling the Other is universally the Self's temptation. But in the East as in the West (more than in the West), there is something that resists this passion for identity.

After having shown how Japan's frontal resistance to the West westernizes Japan, Takeuchi Yoshimi turns toward the other side of Japanese thought—the side I love, dare I admit it? at the risk of being taken for an "Orientalist," the side of its thought that I have cultivated somewhat by reading Zeami and Dôgen: the true (Heidegger's *authentic*?) awakening comes not from believing there is a path leading to emancipation. The awakening is situated in the unbearable feeling (Heidegger's *anxiety*?) that there is no road to follow.

This is a resistance that merits its name because it frees itself as much as possible from the duplication of that against which it resists, writes Takeuchi, who cites Lu Xun: "Hope cannot be said to exist, nor can it be said not to exist. It is just like the roads across the earth. For actually the earth had no roads to begin with, but when many men pass one way, a road is made."[4]

What is important is not that the *Holzwege* lead nowhere. "Nowhere," for Heidegger, is still nonetheless the clearing of Being, in the wood of that which is

---

4. Cited by Naoki Sakai, p. 503.

(*l'étant*). What is important is that, in the desert, where there is neither shade nor undergrowth, there is also no clearing and no road that leads to it. So it is, in the dependence of this clarity, in Japan as well as in the West, that one resists the metaphysics of empire, whether Occidental or Oriental.

concealments

chapter 8

The General Line

for Gilles Deleuze

"From the earliest days of my youth I had had the notion that every person has his own no-man's-land, a domain that is his and his alone. The life everyone sees is one thing; the other belongs to the individual, and it is none of anyone else's business. By that in no way do I mean to imply that, from an ethical standpoint, one is moral and the other amoral, or, from that of the police, one licit and the other illicit. But man lives at intervals unchecked, in freedom and in private, alone or with someone, be it for an hour a day, an evening a week, or a day a month; he lives for that private, free life of his from one evening (or day) to the next: those hours exist in a continuum.

"Those hours either complement something in his visible life or else possess some independent significance. They may be a joy or a necessity, or a habit, but they are crucial to demarcating any sort of 'general line.' If a man does not exercise this right of his, or if because of extenuating circumstances this right is denied him, he will one day wake up to find that he has never really found himself, and there is something depressing in that."

The right to this no-man's-land is at the very foundation of human rights.

The narrator of *The Revolt* knows this when she adds: "An inquisition or a totalitarian state, incidentally, can never allow this second life, which eludes any and every control."[1] In *1984*, George Orwell told the story of one man's resistance to the annihilation of his second life by the powers that be.

Humanity is only human if people have this "no-man's-land." There, one is not necessarily in solitude. "Alone or with someone," everyone can "meet oneself there." There is room for several in the second life, me, you, the other.

On the other hand, "it's wrong to think of that other life, that no-man's-land, as a luxury, and everything else as normal. That's not where the dividing line falls. It falls along the line of absolute privacy and absolute freedom," the same voice specifies.

Nor is this really more about some right to secrecy. The secret authorizes that at the moment one not say what one knows. But "the secret existence" is "free," because you don't know what should be said. You grant your hours of solitude to that existence because you have a need not to know more. That's how it is that you

---

1. Nina Berberova, *The Revolt*, trans. Marian Schwartz (London: William Collins Sons & Co, 1989), pp. 27–28.

can encounter what you are unaware of. However, you wait for it. And you can try to make it come. You read, you drink, you love, you make music, you give yourself over to the ritual of your little obsessions, you write. But these means to provoke the encounter are also part of this mysterious region. They keep the secret and nothing assures that they will work.

The region is secret because it is separate. The right to the second existence is the right to remain separate, not to be exposed, not to have to answer to someone else. They used to say: to keep one's self-containment (*quant à soi*). (But one's self, you precisely don't know what it is. One's something-containment [*quant-à-quelque chose*].) This right ought to be recognized, and respected, for everyone.

Not a self, it's something to encounter. It's surely *no man* because these kinds of moments are not needed to make the acquaintance of *man*. Oneself, one is there only to protect *no man* and to keep guard around one's *land*.

Just because you don't have to answer to others with regard to what goes on in this region, it does not follow that you are irresponsible. It follows only that it happens by means of answers and questions. It is not argued.

Nina Berberova makes her narrator say that these moments "are crucial to demarcating any sort of 'general line.'" The "general line" is not the line of life in general, of life "such as it is." The second existence is nonetheless sweet in relation to "the life everyone sees." It suspends it a little, it dwells within it from time to

time and sweeps it away, but without one knowing anything about it. The second existence does not really
wrong the first one; it opens little parentheses within it.

It's when general life seeks to take hold of the secret
life that things go bad. The human right to separation,
which governs our declared rights, is thus violated.
There is no need for a totalitarian power, or a libelous
rumor, no need to expel, incarcerate, torture, no need
to starve, to prohibit from working or having a home,
to censor, occupy, isolate, or take hostage, in order to
violate the right to separation.

These are, of course, good, ostensible, direct, and
infallible means to intimidate the guard who watches
over the second existence, to weaken that existence,
make it harder, invade it and annex it to general life.
This is undoubtedly because the masters of general life,
whoever they might be, are thus haunted by the suspicion that there is something that escapes them, that
might plot against them. They need the whole soul, and
they need this soul to surrender unconditionally.

There is a more imperceptible procedure, one that
insinuates itself better, without overt violence, into the
white or gray region where everyone separates oneself
from other humans and gropes one's way forward along
one's own general line. This insinuation does not at all
have the air of a terror. The appeal to human rights, to
declared rights may very well legitimate it and give it
cover. Express yourselves freely, have the courage of your
ideas, of your opinions, communicate them, enrich the
community, enrich yourselves, set yourselves to it, con-
verse, there is nothing but good in making use of your

rights since it takes place in respecting the rights of others, circulate, everything is possible within the limits fixed by laws or rules. And besides, these rules can themselves be revised.

I speak in this way about liberal democracies, about "advanced" societies where human rights are recognized and respected as much as possible, in any case always remembered and defended, and little by little extended to all those who, in North America, are called by the name of minorities. These commandments of liberal democracy are good. They allow, and even request, Amnesty International to exist. They allow, when the opportunity offers, little reflections like these to be published without difficulty. Whoever is not in agreement with them can always dispute them.

That doesn't keep the repeated invitation to exert one's rights and to watch over their observance from being a pressure to the point of oppression. A little increase in pressure, and that will be the end of secret hours. Everyone will be snapped up by others, by responsibilities, absorbed in defending the proper use of rights in general life, enticed away from one's guard upon the "general line" that belongs to one.

For the exercise of one's rights and the vigilance over their being respected to be required as forms of duty, therein lies a kind of self-evidence, as infallible as a totalitarian disposition can be. Infallible as for the ruin of self-containment. Why didn't you do this, say that, you had the right!

Bergson said that no one was obligated to write a book. The care involved in writing books comes back to that existence in which everyone lives "unchecked," even by one's own self. Writing is one of the means, necessarily risky, of making an encounter. One writes because one does not know what one has to say. But today's slogan is: *Publish or perish!* If you are not public, you disappear; if not exposed as much as possible, you don't exist. Your no-man's-land is interesting only if expressed and communicated. Heavy pressures are put on silence, to give birth to expression.

Does this pressure affect only writers, "intellectuals"? Not at all, anyone else at all has the same duty to use his or her right to be informed and heard. Everyone must be able (to exercise the right) to bear witness. Institutions see to it that we are all stationed on the edge of ourselves, turned toward the outside, benevolent, ready to listen and to speak, to dispute, to protest, to explain ourselves. Through inquiries, interviews, polls, roundtables, "series," "case files," we see ourselves in the media as humans busy fulfilling the duty to assert our rights.

They repeat to us: no problem, everything is possible. A law has been legislated for your case. If not, they'll institute it, you will be authorized. They'll even help you use it as a recourse. All that is well and good, who would dare to complain? Surely not those deprived of legal means. This pressure makes general life more just and attentive.

This life is not without "melancholy," however. It is true that we owe others respect for their rights and that they owe us a respect for ours. And that everyone owes it to him or herself to be absolutely respected. But there is in this self another, whomever or whatever the self meets or seeks to meet during the hours of secrecy. This other exerts an absolute right over the self that was never contracted and is unaware of reciprocity. It is utterly other than "the others." It requires our time and our space in secret, without giving us anything in exchange, not even the cognizance of what it is, or what we are. We have no rights over it, no recourse against it, and no security.

Now, all busy with legitimating exchanges in a community with others, we are inclined to neglect the duty we have to listen to that other and to annul the second existence it requires of us. And so to become ourselves perfectly interchangeable, without remainder, within the conditions of public and private law.

In what, thereupon, would we still be respectable? Rights and respect for rights are owed to us only because something in us exceeds every recognized right. The latter has only the final sense of safeguarding what is found beyond or below it. Misery, sin, unconsciousness, suffering, shame, or inspiration, energy, passion, grace, and talent, what do we know about it?

If humanity does not preserve the inhuman region in which we can meet this or that which completely escapes the exercise of rights, we do not merit the rights that we have been recognized. Why would we have the right to freedom of expression if we had nothing to say but the already said? And how can we have any chance of finding how to say what we know not how to say if we do not listen at all to the silence of the other within? This silence is an exception to the reciprocity of rights, but it is its legitimation. The absolute right of the "second existence" must be well recognized, since it is that which gives the right to rights. But as it escapes rights, it must always be content with an amnesty.

chapter 9

A Bizarre Partner

I'm proposing to enter into the American discussion here. And maybe into *the* discussion, the one that's been going on for the last two decades in the heart of the Western intellectual community, including Japan. "French thought" is present in it, but these debates seem almost entirely absent from the thought of people in France. It is important, and difficult, to analyze the motives for the French resistance to this international discussion. You might say that the intellectual propositions that come to us from elsewhere seem to us (when they do get to us, I mean, when by dint of translations and presentations, they happen to penetrate into the interior of the Hexagon) to be either deprived of interest on their own terms, or in answer to questions already thought through by us, or insufficiently worked out, or finally badly framed. I believe we sincerely think that the real questions are not subject to argumentation and that writing is the only thing that can *embrace* them.

I intend here, justly, to argue, in the international and especially "American" manner, the limits "French" writing opposes to argumentation. I will confine myself to some of the questions raised during a debate I engaged in with Richard Rorty at the Johns Hopkins University in 1984 and published in the journal *Critique* (no. 456), thanks to Vincent Descombes, under the title "La traversée de l'Atlantique" (Crossing the Atlantic). This is not to say that other questions seem less important to me, far from it.

To begin with, let me take the occasion of Richard Rorty's twin judgment on the "philosophy" of language inherent in the language of respectively Anglo-American and French philosophers. Rorty first admitted that Anglo-Saxon (read: traditional) philosophers hold an "implausible position" when "they claim that everyone has always spoken the same language, that questions of vocabulary are 'merely verbal,' and that what matters is argumentation." They would do well, he concludes, to become "a little more French." But, on the other hand, he adds: "We Anglo-Saxons consider that French philosophy would gain by admitting that the adoption of a new vocabulary can only take place if we can discuss the weaknesses of the old one and if we can dialectically navigate between the old and the new vocabulary." He concludes: "It seems to us that our French colleagues are too eager to find or create a linguistic island and to invite people to dwell there, and not enough interested in building bridges between these islands and the mainland."

By situating myself, then, within the argumentative

genre and by hoping to contribute to the discussion requested by Rorty, I shall underscore two aspects of the divergence for which the "Atlantic" thus supposedly bears responsibility: first of all, the exact nature of the heterogeneity (or insularity) that concerns me in language, and which *is not* that of vocabularies; and the extension of what neopragmatism calls the pragmatics of language until it reaches a condition that far exceeds that of a discussion leading to consensus, which is how our American colleagues, in my opinion, seem to limit it.

It is accepted, in a discussion, that each of the interlocutors seeks to make the other one share his or her point of view, that is, to persuade that other. And this intention has sense only if the points of view are initially divergent. One wonders, then, how dissent can give rise, in the wake of discussion, to assent or consensus.

In rationalist metaphysics, divergences are thought to issue from prejudices, opinions, passions, particularities, contexts—all of which are forms of error, which discussion comes to dispel by testing them against the light of reason. It is thereby supposed that there is a universal, rational language. Discussion is possible only because each point of view is translatable into this language and because this translation reveals what is erroneous in the particular point of view.

If this strong hypothesis is admitted, then it would be fitting to say that assent is obtained through conviction rather than persuasion. The difference between these two, so-designated procedures has been clearly established since Aristotle, when he distinguished between a state of *épistémè* obtained through logic and a state of *pistis* obtained through dialectical and/or rhetorical procedures. The principle of a universal language is posited as the only legitimate foundation for assent. You are reduced to persuasion when you are not *able* (in dialectics and rhetoric) or when you do not *want* (in rhetoric and sophistics) to use universal language. Pursuing his inquiry into pragmatic procedures, Aristotle isolates still other means to obtain consensual effects, such as poetic or ethical procedures.

These distinctions are maintained, with differing destinies, throughout Western metaphysical thought. Leibniz's thought may be considered an attempt to wholly reabsorb these distinctions within an exclusively convincing language, that of the Mathesis Universalis. But these distinctions are conserved and reinforced by Pascal and Kant. The three *Critiques* correspond to an examination of the conditions proper to three procedures for obtaining assent: cognitive, ethical, and aesthetic. In this regard, the novelty introduced by his criticism resides in the rules for ethical or aesthetic discussion being no less universally valid than those presiding over cognition. But these rules differ from the latter, and they differ among themselves. The unity of reason appears to be destroyed, then, there being several kinds of universality. Two interlocutors, one of whom proceeds to argue following the cognitive rationality defined by Kant, and the other following his/her ethical (or aesthetic) rationality, cannot arrive at a shared conviction, for lack of a common transcendental grammar. All they can do is agree, thanks to the reflective judg-

ment, on the heterogeneity of these thought procedures. Despite the reasonable but misplaced objections
Rorty makes to my reading of Wittgenstein, I still think
that the multiplicity of "language games" sets up an
analogous difficulty, *mutatis mutandis*, to the principle
of a homogeneous language.

Here, I will make two observations on this topic,
destined without a doubt to facilitate a final agreement.
First of all, the question raised by the heterogeneity of
technai, faculties, games, or genres is in no way that of
the ability to *learn the rules* proper to each of these procedures, as Rorty makes me say. Clearly, determining
the rules of a genre is secondary to the usage or practice
of that genre. The interlocution is indeed where the
learning takes place. Still we have to agree on what we
mean by interlocution. I will return to this in closing.

What I'm trying to get at is not learning at all, but
the conditions for assent, that is, the procedure for dis-
pelling the dissent that characterizes the relation between the interlocutors at the beginning of a discussion.
What I'm saying is that dissent is not dispelled in the
same way when we're dealing with solving an equation
to the second degree, judging the beauty of a sculpture,
explaining a physical phenomenon, evaluating the justice of an action, or deciding on a vote during an elec-
tion. This banal observation is so scarcely irrationalist,
as Habermas sometimes pretends to believe, that on the
contrary, I believe it is the only one respectful of the
specificity of reasonable procedures. Rationality is reasonable only if it admits that reason is multiple, as Aristotle said that being is spoken multiply.

Second observation. The problem raised by this multiplicity must be distinguished from the problem of translation. The latter is a problem of language. I find myself in agreement with the critique Donald Davidson makes of the notion of a "conceptual scheme" that would be proper to the idiom of each of the interlocutors (whether individuals or communities) and that would prohibit them from communicating, and *a fortiori* from arriving at a consensus. The notion of such a scheme presupposes, as Davidson shows, some entity, a world, nature, experience, evidence (I would add: universal language) that would exist in and of itself independent of every scheme, that is, of every language, and which this scheme would come to deform or form, order (I would say: fictionalize) in its singular "fashion." But the hypothesis of a scheme would prohibit this entity being described in any way other than by means of a scheme. Wherein this hypothesis turns out to be intrinsically aporetic. And how would I know my interlocutor was using a scheme other than mine, unless I could translate it into my language? The notion of an absolute alterity is in and of itself also aporetic, since alterity is relative to an identity. The points of dissent presupposed in the discussion are thus declared to be always assimilable to divergences expressible within a language and mutually translatable.

As Davidson observes, it does not follow that there is a universal language, for there is no evidence of this unique universality. One need only admit what Davidson calls a principle "of charity," according to which I recognize the disagreement I have with someone by acknowledging that he/she considers the proposition I oppose to be true.

When I invoke the heterogeneity of *technai,* faculties, games, or genres, I can readily admit Davidson's principle of charity. The question of the *linguistic* translatability of sentences exchanged between someone who proceeds cognitively and someone who proceeds ethically or aesthetically is not raised. It's in the very definition of a language that every sentence it allows be translatable into the sentence of another known language.

What does not go without saying, though, even allowing for the principle of charity, is that the procedure by which I seek to "persuade" my interlocutor that something is beautiful can be translated into the procedure by which my interlocutor seeks to persuade me that this same something is true.

It serves no purpose to argue that we are, of course, precisely not talking about the same thing. For the discussion itself is what says so, and no external third party can know it in advance. (I'm thinking incidentally about that subject that has not yet been given to the function of the "rigid designator" elaborated by Saul Kripke, namely the role it takes in the fixing of the referents to be discussed. But I'll drop this.)

Grant me, in fact, that within the hypothesis of a discussion in which the stakes are not the same for each of the two interlocutors, consensus appears impossible to obtain. But it should also be added that this hypothesis is inept, since it would put us in the case of a "dialogue between the deaf."

What is interesting in this objection is that the notion of "stakes" must be introduced. This corresponds precisely to Wittgenstein's conception of a language game. The procedures for discussion or argumentation are dependent on the stakes. In the Anglo-American tradition, these stakes are brought back to an intention. But I note that, in transcribing what I call stakes as intention, the homogenization of stakes is authorized. It will be said in effect that in every case of discussion, everyone aims to persuade the other that what he or she says is true. The procedure of persuasion, according to Rorty, and the imputing to the other that he/she believes in what he/she says, according to Davidson, are thus authorized by a kind of universal self-evidence, as if in effect discussing or conversing in every case presupposed only a single intention, that of *persuading* the other of my *veracity*. This is to admit but a single procedure, persuasion, and a single set of stakes, veracity.

This exclusiveness is not without analogy with what happens in speculative thought. The analogy consists in substituting a sentence in quotation marks for a sentence without them. I say that *The Bar of the Folies-Bergère*, a painting by Manet, is beautiful. My Davidsonian interlocutor understands me to say that it is true for me to say that "*The Bar of the Folies-Bergère* is beautiful," or "The beauty of this painting is true for me." Such is my interlocutor's charity, a wholly philosophical one you see, not metaphysical of course, but meta-argumentative. And my Rortian interlocutor understands that I am preparing to persuade him/her *of that veracity*. For how *could I persuade* this interlocutor by an argument about the beauty of the painting itself, which is no more than a sentiment I feel upon seeing it? At the risk here of bringing the neopragmatist ire down on me, let me recall Kant's antinomy of taste: "(1) Thesis. The judgment of taste is not based upon concepts, for otherwise it would admit of controversy (would be determinable by proofs). (2) Antithesis. The judgment of taste is based on concepts, for otherwise, despite its diversity, we could not quarrel about it (we could not claim for our judgment the necessary assent of others)" (*Critique of Judgment*, § 56).

As soon as I discuss the beauty of the *Bar of the Folies-Bergère*, I admit Rorty and Davidson's requisites. And just by that I admit that it is an affair of concepts, hence of truth and persuasion, following the meaning they give those words. But then the sentiment of a painting's beauty is treated as if it were "exponible" (ibid., § 57), that is, as if it could be translated into concepts and argued. The heterogeneity between taste and certitude is thereby lost, and the difference between aesthetics and dialectics, or between the beautiful and the true, disappears.

I will not elaborate on the argument by which Kant attempts to break out of this aporia. It suffices for me to show with the help of this aporia how the principle (political in Rorty's case, linguistic for Davidson) that discussion is always possible comes up against a problem. This problem in no way derives from the heterogeneity of untranslatable idioms, be they individual or cultural, but it resides in the irreducibility of one genre of discourse to another, be it within the discourse of a single speaker or between two interlocutors speaking the same language.

This irreducibility is, of course, not of such a kind that the interlocutor who "speaks aesthetics" cannot understand the one who "speaks cognition." On the contrary, I would say, picking up on Davidson's argument, that it is because that interlocutor is able to speak in a variety of ways, or if you prefer, because his/her language allows completely different stakes and procedures that the differend is possible. The fact of the differend is in no way refuted by objecting, as Manfred Frank does, that the differend requires a common language. Simply put, this word language is understood so broadly that it allows for every kind of slippage. I take the word here as meaning a natural language, which is by definition translatable into another that is already known.

My interlocutors often take *language* in the sense of an idiom, a theory, even a culture. I'm willing to accept these meanings with the exception, nonetheless, of the sense of theory. My point is that this natural language or this cultural particularity includes within it different stakes, and that it allows a number of different genres of pragmatic procedure, that is, of action upon the interlocutor. What is said about something in the aesthetic genre can be transferred to the cognitive genre thanks to metalanguage, which consists in putting the aesthetic sentence between quotation marks. But these transferences are never translations. Rather, they should be called "referrals."

(I except theory from the meanings of the word

language that seem allowable to me, because theory belongs entirely only to the cognitive genre. That's why, moreover, the incommensurability of scientific paradigms, such as Thomas Kuhn believes he can conclude from his analysis of the history of science, appears unacceptable to me.)

If the fact of these heterogeneities is admitted, it follows that we cannot accept discussion directed toward persuasion, nor even "conversation," as the minimal pragmatic state. Rorty thinks that discussion is the only alternative to violence and that the mere intention to persuade is sufficient to bring more and more speakers into the community of interlocutors. The notion of a conversational minimum is surely indispensable to liberal, democratic politics. This is nothing new. I don't see what can be opposed to it if we agree that there is no political alternative to liberal democracy, as seems to me from now on to be the case. That's why I don't think it's fair for Rorty or others to authorize themselves to hear resonances of leftism, revolution, or even terrorism, in my defense of the differend.

It's one thing to consider discussion, or even "mere" conversation, in view of spreading consensus as an important political task, and quite another to reduce every "usage" (if one may spare me the word), every use that can be made of language to it. I have two observations to make on this subject.

First, it seems certain to me that even in politics, discussion, in the Aristotelian sense of dialectic, is not everything. Other genres of discourse necessarily intervene (rhetoric, ethics, jurisprudence), about which it is not true to say that every sentence can be concluded from a discussion, or are even subject to discussion. For example, there is no political community without a supreme ideal, or I would rather say, without a supreme obligation. Should we be the richest, the most national, the most powerful, the happiest, the most egalitarian, etc.? Trying to conclude the answer to this question of *duty* from a descriptive argument is completely vain. Argumentation can do nothing more than elaborate the procedures by which, once the ideal has been decided, the interlocutors constituting the community have the greatest chance of collectively coming close to it. John Rawls's analysis of justice, for example, does not discuss what answer may be given to the question of duty. This question is given from the start: justice is distributive equality. Rawls's theory of justice consists only in discussing the procedures that allow for best assuring equality in the distribution of goods, that is, advantages and inconveniences of all kinds, between individuals and groups. But, as John Rajchman notes, it is not demonstrated, nor can it be demonstrated, that distributive equality is what is just. And this is also what in other terms Ernest Nagel sets forth in opposition to Rawls's theory.

At the limit, a duty (also called a principle, in a highly uncertain way) will be admitted just when no interlocutor can reasonably reject it. The contractualism Thomas Scanlon defends thus turns consensus, or more exactly, turns the impossibility of reasonable dissent concerning an obligation, into the very content of that obligation's justice. As Scanlon writes, "the idea of general agreement [is] what morality is about" ("Contractualism and Utilitarianism," in *Post-Analytic Philosophy*, ed. John Rajchman and Cornel West [New York: Columbia University Press, 1985], p. 241).

This is as much as to say that the normative value of an obligation comes from its not being debatable by any reasonable argument. Here, rational discussion or argumentative give-and-take is itself set up as the ideal of justice. The way to proceed takes the place of what is supposed to be attained by the procedure. This is a pre-eminent case of one genre being invaded by another, in particular of ethics and law by the cognitive, in the Aristotelian sense of dialectics. But this invasion can only take place thanks to the equivocation that reigns over what is or is not reasonable to reject in the matter of justice. Which reason are we talking about?

In the second *Critique* or in *The Metaphysics of Morals*, Kant too invokes the unanimity of practical reasonable beings in the formation of the moral law, but only so as to guide or direct singular ethical judgments. What is just will be decided, *so dass, als ob, as if* that decision must be able to be accepted by everyone as the maxim of a legislation. This acceptability is not the content of what is just, but a procedure to be mentally followed within a "determination" that can only be done case by case and by analogy. For duty must first be felt as undetermined, that is, deprived of content, for the very condition of morality (freedom) to be satisfied. It must present itself as an initially empty obligation. The sign of its presentation is not a concept, but a sentiment, that of respect. It's up to free reflection to give a content to what is owed. Without this initial emptiness, reason would cease being practical, since it would leave no place for responsibility. If a law were knowable, ethics could be resolved into a procedure of cognition.

I will turn now to the second observation relative to this preeminence of discussion over all other "usages" of language. My reservations bear upon the pragmatic axis itself, which I prefer to call the axis of address. It is admitted that, in a discussion, the locutor and allocutor are in a position of interlocution. That means that the *I* and *you* (or *we* and *you*) poles are held in turn by individuals, as they say in the Anglo-American tradition, or by groups, I believe it would be more prudent to say by bearers of proper names, who are also they who do the discussing. So it is that a *we* is in sum preconstituted within the very rules of argumentation. It is proper to discussion that the *we* be pre-given in a structural fashion. The name bearers admit a priori that they are permutable within the exchange of pronouns. A *we* encompasses *I* and *you* (or *we* and *you*) by principle, since the pragmatics of argumentation presupposes the commutability of names along the poles of destination. This is the situation that authorizes Rorty to place his bets on discussion, in order to extend the *we* to all possible proper names, be they Cashinahua or Martian. I can describe this situation, without departing from Rorty's thought, by saying that it implies, at the level of the rule of commutability, a kind of interlocutory pre-consensus.

But it is erroneous to think that all genres of discourse offer the same disposition, which seems to me, on the contrary, proper to the epistemic or dialectical genre where *me* and *you* (or *us* and *you*) discuss what meaning to give a referent. It is clear that the pragmatic situation is wholly other when it is a matter of making believe (which is what rhetoric reserves for itself under the heading of persuasive eloquence), to make tremble, cry, or laugh (as in poetics or aesthetics), or to make happen (prescription in general).

I'll go even farther, at the risk of irritating our American friends. I wonder what the disposition of the pragmatic axis is when it is a matter of those "genres" that are called writing, reflecting—and I will add, translating, which is far from being reducible to the operation of putting one language in communication with another. In these "genres"—it being understood that this word does not designate genres, literary or otherwise, that are already endowed with their own set of stakes and rules—in these "usages" of language, which are really battles with, against, and within the words of languages, I doubt that interlocution and its rule of commutability are what organizes the pragmatic relation. Rather, we should ask ourselves to whom are addressed the sentences that take shape under the pen of a Montaigne, a Shakespeare, a Kafka, a Joyce, or a Gertrude Stein, or also a Spinoza or a Wittgenstein. Whatever the name one finds to designate their *you* in the singular or the plural, grant me that in any case, the relation between he or she who writes or reflects and he or she who is supposed to be the addressee will not be interlocutory.

I am trying to show this in terms acceptable to neopragmatism. It's known that new individuals or bearers of proper names never stop coming one after the other, in the course of time, to present themselves in that place (the addressee's) left empty by the—shall we call it, literary—work of art. They come, in sum, to *listen* to it, to read it, criticize it, comment upon it. To send it to themselves. Here, I am disregarding the variety of ways they can listen to it and situate themselves as addressees. But in every case, the situation of reading differs profoundly from that of discussion. In discussion, the argumentation increasingly adjusts how what was said at the beginning is heard, a process that tends to draw the points of view of addressor and addressee closer together, the horizon of this convergence being their consensus. In the *écoute* of writing or reflection, divergence rather is what is expected. The work accepts or even requires its being heard in every possible manner. It cannot bear that one "method" of reading imposes itself over all others, assigning the work a definitive meaning and allowing it to be classified once and for all. On the contrary, the work expects what Harold Bloom terms a *misreading*, an *écoute* that diverges from established traditions. This is also what Rorty writes in *Consequences of Pragmatism*: "We don't *want* works of literature to be criticizable within a terminology we already know; we want those works and criticism of them to give us *new* terminologies" (p. 142).

I will set aside all that is excessively voluntarist and perhaps experimentalist in this description. I would like to hold onto one implication.

If a work requires a new vocabulary from criticism, this is because it disturbs the critical tradition. The work is not addressed to that criticism, since it troubles it. To whom is it then addressed, that its consequence is to displace? Obviously, the only criticism that can attempt to say it is one that does not remain tributary to tradition alone.

I would go even farther: a "bad reading" does not need to *say* who is the work's addressee, for it will have first tried to *be* that addressee. If something can be said about the work that has not yet been said, then it is because it is listened to otherwise. In this other *écoute* resides the respect one owes to writing and to thought. It's not that one seeks to be innovative. All that is supposed is that the work's destination is sufficiently indeterminate for determinations other than those that are known to remain possible.

There is, therefore, in the work of writing and thought a pragmatic indeterminacy or an indeterminacy of destination. The addressor, the writer or the thinker, does not and did not know to whom or what is addressed what he or she writes or thinks. That addressor knew only one thing, which formulated pragmatically, is that he/she *had to* write and think as he/she did. He/she also knows that the finished work is not at the level of this duty. He/she remains in a state of debt. The undetermined addressee who ordered the work remains unsatisfied by what was delivered, and the author remains in the addressee's debt. So it is too that the addressor remains in the debt of all his or her later addressees, readers, critics, and commentators who, in their attempts to propose *écoutes* for the work, put themselves in the place of its possible addressee.

In regrouping all these traits that proceed, let me recall, from *misreading* alone and that by themselves explain the need for "new terminologies," I come to the conclusion that the addressee of writing and thought presents all the characteristics of a non-empirical entity, empty if you will, and transcendent to every "real" destination and denomination. Were there not this jealous and angry entity to call upon the author, the latter would be neither a writer nor a thinker. And the work would be a great work only if it asked for an infinity of always possible *écoutes* after having been written. Here, we touch upon the limits of an argumentative pragmatism. The other who is at play in the kind of work Rorty or Bloom call for is not an interlocutor with whom the author must change places along the instances of *you* and *we*. I think if Rorty himself, to deal only with him, writes and thinks, even just to signify that discussion is the only important thing, it is because he too is taken hold of by a duty that was never the object of a discussion nor of a contract, or to put it otherwise, because he is held hostage by an other who is not his interlocutor.

Let me finish his remark by a wish: which is that pragmatism study pragmatics a bit more. It will find, first of all, that it is "internal," if I may say so, as much as external, insofar as each so-called individual is divisible and plausibly divided into a number of partners—which is, when all is said and done, what Freud has taught us at least for almost a century and which cannot reasonably be ignored. Let me add that there is no need—quite the contrary—to accept Freud's metaphysics, which he called his metapsychology, to recognize the plurality of addresses, and the plurality in the nature of those addresses, which make up the tissue of this "internal" pragmatics.

Through this effort of intelligence, which has nothing to do with the "application of a theory," pragmatism would also discover that there is no need to be Lacanian to allow, for example, at least as a "perishable" tool, the division between the imaginary, the symbolic, and the real. How can the real not be recognized in the other that I have called, out of provocation, transcendental and that imposes a debt of writing and thought? How can all the nameable, empirical, or possible interlocutors that Rorty's progressivism yearns to introduce into discussion not be seen to be figures of the imaginary? And how could Rorty himself refuse to agree that his pragmatic minimum, discussion, operates as the symbolic minimum necessary for the institution of the community to take place?

To end, let me return to the question of the differend's resolution, by asking it from the point of view of the preceding implication. Rorty writes in the text he read at Hopkins in 1984: "Political liberalism comes down to suggesting that one tries to substitute litigation for differends as much as possible, and that there is no philosophical reason a priori for this effort not to succeed, just as . . . there is no reason a priori for this effort to achieve its end."

This is what I would respond: there is a philosophical reason a priori for a litigation to be substituted for a differend, and there is a philosophical reason a priori for that substitution to leave intact language's potential for differends.

The first reason stems from the ability of every sentence to put itself or let itself be placed between quotation marks. This ability is the very one we use (if I may be allowed his word too) in discussion, among many others, as I hope I showed at the beginning.

The second reason stems from the ability every sentence has to be linked with another according to heterogeneous ends. As Wittgenstein says, you can play tennis, chess, or bridge. The same is true for language: you can "play" at the true, the just, or the beautiful. You could say that every game has the same end, that of winning. But this is false. All by herself, a child plays with pieces of fabric, with no particular end in mind. Writers, too, with their fabrics of language.

Comparing genres with games is only valid, obviously, if we admit that the same words or the same sentences can be treated sometimes as tennis balls, or as chess pawns, or playing cards, or bits of fabric.

This being the case, the question of translating one sentence into another, I repeat, poses no particular problem (unless it be that of translation itself, which is an immense one. Maybe it's the most obscure language game of all). But translating the "employment" of a sentence with one aim into its employment with another is impossible. *Mutatis mutandis*, you may utilize tennis balls or playing cards or fabrics in the place of chess pieces, but the moves you impress upon the balls used as pawns are not those you impress when you play tennis with them. I refer to these moves as links. They are nothing more than modes of associating words or sentences. But these modes are heterogeneous. It is false to bring them all back to varieties of rhetoric, or to confuse them with the grammar of a language.

Let's accept now that you are beginning to play with the tennis balls in someone's company. You are surprised to observe that this other person does not seem to be playing tennis with these balls, as you thought, but is treating them more like chess pieces. One or the other of you complains that "that's not how you play the game." There is a differend.

When I ask what is the tribunal that will judge the complaint, I am doing nothing more than following out the metaphor already implied in the very term differend. You must not object, as Rorty does, that I am invoking a judge armed with "pre-established criteria." There are such judges only for a game whose rules have been more or less fixed, after the fact, of course, such as chess or tennis. But under the circumstances, you and your partner must decide what game you are playing or wish to play with the balls.

This is as far as the comparison goes. For balls do not talk balls. But words and sentences can be taken in reference and also refer to their mode of linking. Language, we tell ourselves, is self-referential. You ask the other what game he or she is playing.

Democratic liberalism intervenes then. It declares that it is a good thing for the other to respond and for the discussion to be engaged. In the absence of your interlocution, your partner continuing to play his/her game and you yours, you will not be able to continue to play together. I agree with this. In exploring the nature of the game that you and your partner intend to play, you situate this game as a reference to your discussion (you make a "referral"). Litigation replaces your differend, and you are able to come to an agreement about the way to proceed. But it remains to be proved that it is always *better* to play together. With their bit of fabric, the little girl and the writer invent or discover many things. The question of *Einsamkeit* or *loneliness* needs to be taken up again in terms that far exceed the way in which Wittgenstein interrogates *private language*.

To return to my own argument, you might object that the writer and the little girl are solitary only as "individuals," but that, in their intimacy, several partners, conscious or not, are engaged in their play, and that they are thus having an internal discussion.

But what do we know? We can say they are *discussing* on the inside only if we postulate that the dissent between intimate partners never exceeds litigation. That is to say, only if we admit that the little girl and the writer suffer only hesitations or contradictions that can be solved by an inner debate. This is what the very notion of the individual presupposes.

I suppose that this can take place in effect. But there is no reason a priori to eliminate the other case, which is that of a differend between intimate partners. Resituated on the "outside," the latter case would be more or less as follows: you are playing tennis with the balls, your partner is playing a game you don't know with them. You ask what it is that he/she is playing, *he/she doesn't answer you.* What is it reasonable to do?

I think what is reasonable is to try to learn the other's game. This is what the little girl and the writer are doing within their respective differends. Writers try to arrange words and sentences as they presume their mute "interlocutor" arranges them. This is called writing, and I could say as much for thought. If something new surfaces as the event of a work within thought or writing, this can only be within this pragmatic disorder.

By disorder, I mean only this: that none of the conditions for a free discussion, whether intra- or inter-individual, about an identified object is met. In this sense, one can speak of violence. Violence does not at all consist of the presence of police officers in the room who would constrain one of the interlocutors to accept, under threat, the thesis or game of the other. Violence stems from this dilemma: either you reject the unknown game of your partner, you even reject the fact that it is a game, you exclude it, pick up your balls, and seek a valid interlocutor; and this is a violence done to the event and to the unknown of such a kind that you stop writing or thinking; or else, you do violence to yourself in trying to learn the moves that you don't know and that your silent partner imposes upon the balls, I mean upon the words and sentences. This is called the violence of learning to think or write, which is implied in every education.

I believe this violence is inevitable, because I believe the encounter with this bizarre partner is inevitable.

Moreover, I believe this encounter to be constitutive, on the same level that the encounter with an unnameable addressee is inevitable for a work. It is even plausible that this addressee and this partner are one and the same. But what do we know?

All of this, you, my interlocutors, are quite able to understand, we can have a discussion about it, elaborate it together, and perhaps arrive at a consensus about that other. We can come to agreement on such sentences as: "Yes, there is a bizarre partner; yes, there is an unnameable addressee," etc. But this assent is possible only because that partner, that addressee, that other is precisely not ours while we are discussing. The discussion eliminates that other a priori, since it is not an interlocutor. The discussion can only admit it as a third person, as that about which we discuss. This is what I call placing between quotation marks. We *cite* that other to come forth (*comparaître*). But, at the very moment we are dealing with that other, in writing or in thinking, it in no way *comes forth* (*comparaît*): it barely even *shows forth* (*paraît*) and is barely even in our *company* (*compagnie*). How can we be liberal democrats with such an other?

Consequently, I conclude that it is not more reasonable to make the order of litigation rule over the disorder of the differend, than vice versa. Increasing the capacity to discuss is good; an increasing passibility to the event is just as good.

I leave for the reader to draw from this conclusion that fashion he/she judges appropriate to deal with trans-Atlantic relations. As for me, I think the "mainland"

Rorty wishes for is not desirable in itself. It would be, it already is, occupied by the Empire of meta-conversation, by communicational pragmatics. Keeping watch over our archipelago seems to me to be a wiser disposition. I'm talking about heterogeneous "games" or "genres" of discourse. In America as in Europe, the secret ocean that bathes them is the language of reflection.

chapter 10

Directions to Servants

Andrew Benjamin asks me for a short—very short—preface for his *Lyotard Reader*, nothing at all, four or five pages. Just like that, in passing. As if it went without saying. When nothing goes without saying in this *Lyotard Reader*, nor in the principle that Lyotard himself should write a preface for this *Reader*. You say: *Foreword*. You want him to make a word before his words. A key word, which will give the *reader* the key to the words of the *Reader*.

It's held, it happens that I hold, that the one who writes, the scripter, in a few rare cases the writer, is *his/her own first reader*. This priority or primacy of reading within writing can be supported. It is in appearance coherent. You cannot write without reading yourself. Without rereading yourself, of course, but first of all, without reading yourself. You hear yourself write, obviously. Even if you try not to listen to yourself.

It happens that you listen to yourself write. This is

something other than hearing yourself write. When you hear, you hear only something that has to be written. You don't get to it. You keep on going. You don't worry too much about the manner. You have confidence in it, in the manner. You are ahead of the writing, you are just tracing out its direction. You set the heading. It will follow. It will take care of itself.

When you listen to yourself write, it happens that you don't have confidence in the manner. You strap it down, make it severe, classical, academic. You argue. You address someone. Or, on the contrary, you neglect it in the sense that you get attached to what appears neglected, *négligé*. I would like to defend that *écoute*, which has bad press among censors. It signals that you are not quite sure of the heading, that you are a little or very lost, that you are afraid, that you don't feel you have enough force to think. And that is quite simply just and honest. Not only that you feel this unworthiness, this anxiety, but to signal it by too much writing, a severe or a neglected style. That irritates the reader. But his/her anger is good. It is of the same variety as the unrest of the one who writes. Nor does that person find oneself again either. Overwritten, unreadable.

It also happens, it seems, that you don't listen to yourself while writing. That you lend an ear only to what comes along. It's a grace, for everyone, for those who write and those who read. It's grace. The bliss of writing. However, it's also a great mistake, a presumption, a blind confidence in writing. You act as if you were destined only for the most noble works of thought. You leave to servants the task of making order out of what just thought itself, up ahead of the line of writing. On the edge of words in the process of taking shape, at their point of contact with the white horizon over which thoughts arise. You leave the vile task of administering what the pen is in the process of disposing to skill, to talent, to the informed reader you already are.

A presumption of this talent, of this grinding, first of all. An order of words that would make itself all by itself, behind your back, while you are walking. And then, the supplementary presumption that you can let yourself be reached alive, in the raw, up close, by what you are trying to think while you write. Thank God, it's never like that, you reread yourself.

You reread yourself ahead of time. You will be reread. The thing to write doesn't show up as ingenuous. It is adorned, sometimes with little, with an epithet, an adverb. Or else an entire sentence comes all of a sudden out of the white. Now, these sentences or these words that come about by themselves may hide the thought that was about to speak itself. You think you recognize that thought in them. They are what you recognize, the thought is what you miss. That's when, instead of hearing it, of properly reading it, as properly as possible, you reread it. Already set in these legible words and sentences. This rereading is a prereading, a *foreword*. It's the despair of the one who tries to hear while writing. It's a sound, lovable or not, easy or difficult, but recognizable, that is made on the verge of thought, that makes you not hear its silence enough, not long enough. The servants cleaned the house too quickly, immoderately, before the thought arrives, to give it a good welcome.

That is to say, on the contrary, to gag and disfigure it. Too much order, too much speech, talent and custom to write.

And then, besides, how do you know that this thought that comes along all set up is not the right one? How can you compare it to what it ought to be? Except by setting up the latter in turn. And that would be it, in any case, for grace and the "bliss" of writing. Or else you have to move the whole house out. Change one's domesticity. Have no confidence in easy circumstances. Hence, once again, to listen to oneself write. To assure oneself of other domestic services. To find less, or more, disciplined servants.

The continual sublation of words is the modesty and probity of thought toward writing. It is an infinite endeavor, like translation. How that labor called "correcting," which is just as well uncorrecting from the point of view of the recognized and recognizable tongue, can be done, you have no idea. That you have to "correct," to throw away pages in the wastebasket, substitute one word for another one that is already written and that seemed to do well, that was pleasing, to disavow it, and thereby disauthorize yourself to authorize yourself by another word, perhaps more ordinary or more scholarly, flatter or more unexpected, the one who writes and rereads oneself in order to write "better," always, knows nothing and can know nothing about what the writer does in obeying that duty. What the writer knows is that you don't hear the thought if you don't listen to the words.

Now you imagine an Andrew Benjamin, your

friend, who decides to pick up, from what you have so scribbled over forty years, a few texts for his sole convenience. And to put them together for publication in English.

And he comes to tell you: make me a little *foreword* for this collection. Namely, as I have just explained, the thing to avoid above all else, since that is what impedes the thought that has just come. It is to forewarn it. (Everyone knows that *forewords* are *afterwords*. Still you can manage it so that, before or afterwards, the presentation is not too much of a representation.) I must then forewarn you, readers, about (or against?) what has been able to come to me, in the spirit or in the letter. And you, Anglophones.

An Anglophone struggles, in order to think, in the same way as the scripter or writer I have just described, in the midst of a domesticity that is either too zealous or too disorderly. But this is not my domesticity, it belongs to that of another language. And by language, I don't just mean grammar, lexicon, and phonology, but beyond that, the immense web—singular to everyone in every language but also collectively different from one language to another—the immense web of words and sentences in the midst of which and against which the writer strives to make a place for the thought that comes to him or her. His/her culture, as we say, his/her world. I do know the Anglophone thinks, but with another household, another means of setting up and of moving house.

His/her thought is translatable as much as mine, because languages are translatable by definition. Hence, his/her manner is also translatable. But it is difficult to distinguish in the manner of a foreign text where it sets up its language and where it moves it out. Because that means that you know not only his/her *home* but also how he/she inhabits it. Now, everyone inhabits differently, that's one's singularity. And it may be, moreover, that from one language to the next, the spectrum of ways to inhabit is not the same, at least it doesn't quite cover here what it is there. Hard to know.

What you do know is that you are not at home when you are at the other's. That you are not comfortable in thinking, in making order and disorder. That you have a poor mastery of the reread and the not yet read, representation and presentation and appresentation. That you don't really succeed in listening to the servants. I've had this experience, hardly exemplary of course, on account of my English, for having dared to write in English. And I was even given assurances that my text would be reread before publication by an Anglophone, who would also be a friend of mine. Given assurances that this friend, David Carroll, would laugh at my English, but in a good-natured way, and would make use of his competence, his intelligence, and his time so that the Anglophone reader does not laugh too much. So that the only laughter would be that occasioned by the content.

Was Carroll a translator in this matter? No, he was correcting my English. Coauthor? He didn't write the book. Rewriter? He did not alter the tone, or resituate the text according to a norm determined by the editor-in-chief or series director. Corrector? As it happened, he didn't correct proofs, only the language. We could baptize him as a *co-writer*, a futuristic skill in the cosmopolitan or Babelian situation where we find ourselves. A situation where the *writer* or the *writing agent* is straight off addressing allophones. Where this address is therefore necessarily awkward. It's an allographic situation, a clumsy circumstance (*une circonstance de maladresse*).

As for the household, the allograph will have a lot to do, one might say! With that foreign language that doesn't work all by itself behind him/her to make itself right and proper. That foreign language, on the contrary, never stops telling something other than what wants to be said, with wild connotation—not to speak of solecisms and barbarisms. The foreign language revolts and goes astray without its knowing where, when, or how. While rereading *Directions to Servants*, it comes to mind that this house of servants encouraged by Swift to arrogance, fantasy, vandalism, and felony is a good metaphor for my allograph.

The allograph doesn't get to the point of rereading him/herself in the preceding sense. The service personnel who are supposed to clean up after what he is trying to think do it in another language. And a contrary disposition. Between what the master (whom I imagine to be English in Swift's case) thinks and what the commoners (who must be Irish) execute (write), the consequence cannot be good, except by chance. So it is for a Francophone who writes an English he doesn't possess. Whence a particular feeling of irresponsibility. He doesn't reread himself. He knows that it is a waste of time. That he will never succeed in making it better. Only in making it other, again, and God knows which other! A master in despair of mastering and, by this fact, deresponsibilized. I remember my awful experience like an episode of language infantilism or drunkenness.

I come back to translation. This is another case of Swiftian domesticity, but for other reasons. It's not that the translator is a mean servant. On the contrary, he/she may be as zealous as an old chamberlain, as faithful as an incorruptible chambermaid. Like them, a long acquaintance, love of master and mistress, personal integrity, and self-effacement have made the translator capable of maintaining the household as it should be within the commandments he/she receives. Just as if the boss were executing them himself.

Perhaps nothing is as wondrous as a good translation. Because of this abnegation one feels. Much more than for the motives of technical competence. (The latter can never result from the former.) It arouses a moral respect. For someone who was willing and able to prefer what came to the mind of another rather than what could happen to one's own. Not preferring what the other writes as such, once things have been cleaned up, to what he or she, the translator, could write on the same subject. But, if possible, to prefer the thought that comes to another before being cleaned up. Thus, to prefer the other's disorder, if you like, not just to one's own order, but to one's own disorder, the translator's (for just because you're a translator doesn't mean you think or write any the less). A great effect of love. You don't just love what is born in the other, but also what was asking to be born. And you make it, once again, not just born, but asking to be born, in the so-called target language. A good translator doesn't love, doesn't respect just what is thought, but also the "manner of thinking," as one says.

Is the author the judge of this perfection? Of course not, unless, they say, he or she writes perfectly in both languages. Only the perfect bilingual, or better said, the perfect digrapher, whether the author or not, would be the judge. The perfect bilingual is like the absolute ear, a pre-Babelian dream, of a divine audience without residue, to which not one bit of harmony, not one color would be lost. The ideal of an interlinguistic communication that would precisely have no need of translation. This ideal is the ideal of translation. To make itself useless and even impossible, to efface the interlinguistic gap that motivates it.

But, on the contrary, translation is an infinite task, every version of the target text having to be reread and corrected yet again, such that the translator stops not out of satisfaction but out of fatigue. Every translation, be it famous or recognized for unsurpassable, must be done over after a few years.

This is especially so because, like in writing, the grace of the word that seems to come all of its own is suspect and must be placed under suspicion in the name of the very thing that comes with the word, in the adornment of the word. Here, too, there is a desire to restore to the thing that came (but in the case of translation, that came to the mind of another, of the one whom one translates) its precise candor. Its nakedness.

One insists on respecting a frankness, to make thought in its nascent stage broach the travesty of its inscription in language. But not here either does a child ever come naked, not any more than in writing, and language is never cloaked in anything not already formulated. Always badly formulated, however, by the mere fact of its being formulated.

It's in this regard that translation and allography suitably illustrate writing in its relation to rereading. Their example, respectively of extreme fidelity and infidelity, shows that advancing to inscribe is to have pre-inscribed, advancing to writing is to have reread in advance. I don't conclude from this that the writer or scripter who turns toward the white horizon while writing finds a text already made that need only be restored, or if need be translated, in any case to be read straightforwardly. The preread would never be anything then but prejudice.

A text is not what the writer encounters. No more than the translator has to deal with a text. It can be said that both writer or scripter and translator find a thousand texts before them. A texture of texts. Not even a texture, and not even texts, which would be a great order, the convenience of a weaving passing at regular intervals through a chain. The latter's structure, the former's intrigue. The latter's competence, the former's performance. Etc. Writer and translator do not find this beautiful ordering. They do not even find a mere multiplying of that ordering. They find some of the fabric and lint of texts. That is, their culture, be it English, French, or Irish. Their "baggage" of readings, they say, as if all that could fit in a suitcase. The past of their readings, insofar as the words of that past are not present, but disposed to present themselves to the mind of the writer-scripter or of the translator. Their own texts, their own translations being obviously included in the heap, rags among rags, neither more nor less recognizable than the others.

Not all of their past, of course. Bits of it. Those bits that have come around to present themselves or that are just about to present themselves when a word was imposed or imposed itself, as "thought," as to be thought. I mean a topic you were asked to take on (for a colloquium, a conference, a journal, a book). A commission. For instance, Andrew Benjamin commissions a *foreword* from me for the *Lyotard Reader*.

Right away comes the question: what exactly is the commissioned topic? *Foreword*, Lyotard, or *Reader*? Or one of the possible combinations of the three? Each one of the words, each one of the combinations would give rise to writing, reading, rereading, translation, allography, and betrayal.

Or else, nothing is commissioned. Nothing has the air of being commissioned. You write, translate, out of your own head. It happens that you have the air of writing or translating without being commissioned. But that's not true. There is always a word, or some words, most often taken from elsewhere, reread, led astray, which you use not to isolate a semantic field, but which command you to rummage around in the debris of your rereadings (the white horizon) in a certain way. This is good or it goes bad. It's a question of the heading. If it goes bad, you listen to yourself write (and the translator is par excellence the one who cannot write without listening to oneself). If it's good, you don't have time enough, you rush after the bits of text that fly onto your page under your pen, you record quickly, you say to yourself: we'll see, we'll check it later. Save the housecleaning for later.

But even in the case where the bits come along nicely, a housecleaning has already taken place, and there will be a housecleaning to do. Because the housecleaning that was already done will already have been undone, since it's a question of rags. From the household messed up from the sense of your order, to you who write, in the sense of your order. But this house removal is also a setting up of house. The order sabotaged by the mean servants is done by another order. They disobeyed because they obeyed something else. If you are not their master, it's not that they have another one like you, differing from you in name only. Their meanness does not stem from that simple felony of working in reality for someone else. They don't betray you out of respect for another, but by another kind of respect. They are not wearing another livery under their own, the one you claim to be yours. They obey the memory of themselves, with respect to the common folk of thought. Words remember words.

It's another memory, one more faithful than the good one that you, writer or translator, want. The treason of servants who tear up the order of your thoughts, who decommission your commission and your command, is the faithful memory. It's the solidarity of words among themselves, in their civil and disorganized disobedience. They support each other, even while making retreat. The general, the prince is no longer there to arrange them in ranks and make them fight in a frontal assault, moving toward the horizon. They have given ground in helping each other, already wounded in a war already over, in many wars. In as many wars as texts. Only wounded, for they rarely die. They are all ripped to shreds, but the shreds of words are good. The shreds are like the childhood given back to them after they have pretended to obey, to be grown up, and to go into combat. That's how you will find them, already read and lined up by the heads of war (writers, scripters, translators), made illegible by defeat (for every text is a defeat), left to their own devices, hobbling together on crutches, conglomerating into groups of idle survivors, saving their skin. That's your famous baggage. That's your past, that one that doesn't belong to you, but, as it should be, older and other than you. The one who is neither your son nor your father. Who has nothing in particular to do with you.

And you, what shall you be? Their general, with your commission and your command? Their weaver, to put them back in chains and webbing, to weave your text? Their boss, to send their orders to the kitchen? But even if you do this, and even if you can do nothing else (since you have the presumption to think, write, and translate), I repeat that they will only do whatever they want, or almost (a bit obliged to negotiate their rebellion, nonetheless), and that you cannot count on their goodwill. That you must endlessly reread them, perhaps with the hope of correcting them, of better adjusting to your orders the result of their execution of your orders. But that will not come to an end.

Thus, you reread while writing and reread what is written. In both cases, you rewrite. In both cases, more or less, there is allography. Not yet written and already written, it makes little difference. I said: you cannot not listen to yourself write. Listening to oneself is to listen to the sound of the troop of words in disorder. You cannot hear a thought that comes along if you don't listen to this noise, the noise from which thought comes and to which it goes, out of which it emerges and where it tries to enter.

So has every translator in this *Reader* done with his or her French text. So has done the *editor*, Andrew Benjamin, in gathering together these bits of text. And (I hope) the author, Lyotard, with his thoughts. Does the latter have to come back, not to impose his reading commands upon the disordered troop here gathered for transit to Anglophonia, but rather (if he is faithful and sincere) to add a new disorder to it? To add to it the disorienting rout that (for him) perpetually takes the place of thought? This is certainly not necessary, but it's done.

chapter 11

A Monument of Possibles

In placing this colloquium devoted to the museum under the aegis of Alexandria, the organizers offer the mirage of a comparison between the first Western Mouseion and our contemporary museums. But the analogy is misleading. Malraux refutes it on two occasions in *The Voices of Silence*: "at Alexandria the so-called art museum was but an academy" (trans. Stuart Gilbert [Garden City, NY: Doubleday, 1953], p. 640); and "Our resemblances with Alexandria are of the slightest in this modern world which, in a mere hundred years, has been amputated of the dreams Europe had cherished since the age of the cave man" (p. 591; translation modified). What amputation? The so-called modern world is deprived of legitimation, of the very capacity to believe in its legitimacy. The conservation of its own past as well as the past of cultures foreign to it is not at all something that arises out of the imperial obsession that motivated the monumentality of the Lagides' capital city: the entire memory of humanity. The Ptolemies inherited this compulsion from Alexander's delirium, less a passion to conquer than a syncretic messianism: the empire as a mystical museum. Alexandria may have been the first absolute city, the *Urbs* where the whole *Orbs* was to monumentalize itself, sign itself, and comment on itself. So, for a long time, glory in the West became the supernatural made visible within imperial sovereignty. Christianity, as State religion, would obey that Asiatic principle of legitimation in the administration of people and things, transmitting it all the way on up through to the last modern empires.

After a few centuries of convulsions, the figure of the empire has today been rejected in the West, and another idea of glory reigns, one that is secularized, critical, based only on republican virtues, and descended from the free cities of antiquity. When the supernatural is eliminated from the political sphere, the Mouseion, like the Pharos and the Serapeion, loses its symbolic value. And it enters into *our* modern museum, as bearing witness to another age, and perhaps, another writing.

Just as world capitals are plentiful and in competition with each other, so their museums and libraries are also in competition, and none of them claims to gather together the whole memory of civilizations. Not being exhaustive, they know they are destined to be transformed—destined to what Malraux calls metamorphosis.

There is a scientific reason for accepting this incompleteness. Contemporary museums are constituted as research centers, and their inquiry is informed by ancillary sciences and technologies useful for prospecting and establishing new documents. The archive of the age or region under consideration is never considered to be saturated, any more than the repository of facts that a "hard" science attempts to comprehend. It happens, as in every cognition, that the *inventio* of some piece obliges the museum to do a drastic revision of its collections and working hypotheses. From this wholly cognitive dialectics, it follows that only the form of the *progressive museum* is suitable for contemporary installations.

And as the archive is never complete, the *corpus* of pieces never ceases to be extended. The archivist and the curator, on the one hand, and the director of exhibits, on the other hand, must decide what deserves retention and what deserves exhibition. The difficulty is especially acute in the case of ethnographic archives or collections about contemporary Europe, since there is practically no activity that is not already automatically stored there or might not be. I'll spare the inventory of these modes of recording "from the get-go," which span the gamut from military or family record books through electrical and telephone bills, all the way to radio or television recordings passing by tax notices and credit card bills.

What is collected is subjected here to general hypotheses about the aims of the collection, which must serve the purpose of showing or even demonstrating some supposition relative to the meaning of the activities placed in the archive. But the *exhibition* of the data that have been retained must in its turn also make sense. A sense that is not just that of an argument, but a sense derived from the way in which the items are presented, an "aesthetic" sense. The theoretical conception must be inscribed within the visitor's space and time as being not just any motory and perceptive disposition. Curator, archivist, and/or director work like artists in this respect. The richer the material, the more they must invent forms of presentation—as contemporary composers faced with the infinite series of sounds a synthesizer can furnish have free license to order them into "arbitrarily" chosen structures. Daniel Buren was not wrong to see in the director of an art exhibit the only truly exhibited artist. Maybe he wasn't right in getting indignant about it. I don't see how this aestheticization of the presentation can be avoided when the available material begins to proliferate like a world in expansion.

But the epistemic status of research and the aesthetic mode of presentations conceal the necessarily unfaithful essence of monumentation, or better: of museum *monumention*. By this slight barbarism, I'm pointing to the simple fact that anything at all, no matter how small or trivial—Duchamp's urinal—is transformed into a monument the moment it is placed in the museum with its identification tag.

In the word *monument*, there echo two offshoots of a single root: *mon-* and *ment-*. Indo-European languages abound in terms issuing from this root: *mind* and *meaning, meinen, mens* and *memini, dimenticare, memory, mendacity,* and *dementia,* among others. *Monu-mentum,* for *moni-mentum,* is a kind of suitcase-word (Duchamp again). Read one way, it says the mind of a guard; read the other, the guard of the mind. *Mens, mind* is what sounds the alert, what makes *mentio* or *monitum,* and in that alert sense comes forth, *to mean, meinen.*

Without abusing the etymology, Latin *alertis, alerte* recalls what Old French terms *erte,* retained in the Italian expression *all'erta,* on your guard. Without the cry of the alert, mind and meaning are absent or lost in the inert: that's *amentia* or *dementia.*

The museum monumentalizes. It is the mind concerned about what it might have been and done. It sets up and hangs its remainders. It turns them into traces, which are remainders snatched from inattention. The inert is forgotten and leads the *mens* astray, *dimenticare.* The museum recalls the *mens* to itself in a *com-mentatio.* For every event, whether it stems from a practice, a work of art, or an object, bears its own denial (*démenti*), by dint of its passing and disappearing into a remainder it does not retain and of which what it is a remainder is soon no longer known. In erecting the remainder in a rough state, the museum institutes it as trace. It mounts a memory.

One seems well founded in complaining that the monumentalized trace is not faithful to the event that has passed by. That it has lost the "presence" and "vigor" of the practice or the work when it emerged. That's correct. But was it ever in the mind of the museum, in its *mens,* to present what was formerly present "*in vivo*"? The event that is then actual, if it ever was, is doomed to oblivion among its inert remainders. It must be lost

to be rememorialized (*rememoré*) and commented on as
a trace of itself. Only this ascesis is faithful to the retreat
of Being in the time of appearances.

The infidelity of monumentalization or museum-
ization, the mummifying of practices and works for
which we reproach hangings and glass casings are respectful of the evanescence of all that exists. What
would be demented would be to claim an integral resti-
tution of the now that was back then as if it were the
now of right now. A dementia due to an ontological
forgetting: one omits that what happens is deferred and
distanced right off the bat, that being forgotten is part
of what it is. In so doing, you suppress the possibility of
alertness and memory. For the *mens* is nothing other
than *mentio*, and it is so because it is threatened with
oblivion. Forgetting this forgetting is what threatens it
the most.

The forgetting of forgetting does not just set the
stage for realistic scenes, it is essential to all metaphysics:
in striving to present the thing itself, the ultimate foundation, God, or Being, metaphysics forgets that presence
is absent. The bulimia of Western thought is to have
everything present. That was the delirium of Alexandria.
The wisdom of the world is lovable by its imposition of
the distance that separates traces from and unites them
to events, and by its imposition of this distance on the
visitors. Nothing of what is hung up and exhibited in a
museum remains contemporary with the gaze, even if
it is contemporary from a chronological point of view.
This is what is meant, I believe, by what Jean-Louis

Déotte has called the exposit, a deposit extracted from the inert.

Should we conclude that monumention or museumification is a re-writing? That's saying too much or too little. A re-writing is a writing, and every writing is a re-writing. The dimension of recall and regathering that the *re-* prefix indicates and the museum-like nostalgia that envelopes it mark writing as what is always picked up again (*repris*) from or upon what is forgotten in the inert. Writing is to cry out the alert, or to trace the remainder. There is no immediate writing. It *renders* an account, it accounts for what would be lost without it. In rendering it, it makes be what is not, but which passes by, the existence of the event. And except in the metaphysical or realist illusion, it makes existence *be* but as what lacks being.

This is true not just for its object, for what the writing refers to, but also for its subject, the author. Or rather, let's call him or her the signatory. The signatory too must be forgotten in order to be rendered by monumention. And in effect the annihilation of the signatory's presence from the document he/she signs is required of every signature. For a signature is indeed the stamp the stereotyped gesture of a living body sets upon a document. Mummified by a singular twitching of the hand that makes it recognizable, the gesture of signing anticipates the disappearance of that hand and its body and replaces its presence by the name. The name escapes the vicissitudes of presence. Nonetheless, the signature authenticates the fact that the body bearing that name was indeed the one present at the event. The signature presentifies the body's absence and absentifies its presence, as monumental writing does with its referent. The signature too makes a trace, it gives the alert to an existence doomed to oblivion, it prevents it from being forgotten while remarking that it should have been.

Here, my authorization comes from an unpublished text by Dolorès Djidzek on autography. Her motif is of great importance for understanding what follows on the subject of the museum and of Malraux. She shows that nothing is unless it is written, while what merely exists has no being but dissipates into the night of oblivion. Writing takes its being from nothing else but itself, which is why Djidzek calls it autography. As for the *corpus* of objects to which writing refers, writing is what sets it up. As for the body of its so-called author, writing is what founds it. In signing itself with this one's name, writing alone authenticates its objects. And far from incorporating into itself these objects and the author, and from endowing them with its autographical being, it alerts itself, if I may say so, in regards to their non-being and inscribes them according to their precarious exteriority in the distance separating the existent from being.

This distance imposes the future anterior mood onto both objects and signatory: they will have been, they will have done . . . This mood signifies both that they have already disappeared and that they will not disappear. Disappeared as existing, durable as written. They must be written in order not to forget that they are forgotten as existing. Such is the metamorphosis of the remainder into a trace. Trace: the nothingness of the existent is transformed into the being of the nonexistent.

Now, isn't this also the case for the *corpus* made up by the objects in a museum and by the bodies who have left the initials of their name on these objects or their identifying tags? Doesn't the museum maintain both of these in the condition of a melancholic absence, even while exhibiting them? Is the slightest difference to be seen between writing, signing, alerting, and monumentalizing? All four are subject to the rigorous law by which being can only be made by paying tribute to nothingness. Tracing only by leaving some remainder.

Following a rather conventional reversal of perspectives, but one faithful to the future anterior mood, the beginnings of Malraux's opus must be written on the basis of its end. The essential thesis of *The Imaginary Museum* and *The Metamorphosis of the Gods* (1951 and 1977, respectively) is already proposed, under different adornments, in his juvenilia and in his five novels. But it would also be fitting, proceeding in the opposite direction, to show that the extreme nihilism illustrated by the beginnings is precisely what is followed up on and, perhaps, answered by the idea of the museum. And about this answer, I'll have a word in conclusion.

It would not be incorrect to place the early writing under the seal of a double conviction, never to be denied, and which immediately refers to the theme of autography: there is no existence that is worthwhile, or even, that is; writing (often called creation by Malraux) alone makes be what it signs. This *resolute deception*,

which has often been degraded into an episodic conception of the absurdity of the world, is authenticated
by the Nietzschean legacy of Sorel, Barrès, and Gide,
but also, and this is not without interest, by the dark
Christianity of Saint John and Saint Bernard, Pascal,
Dostoyevsky, and Bernanos. This is not without interest
because the tension between the despair brought on by
the century and the promise of its remission, a tension
proper to this Christian current, in effect gives to Malraux's work its singular theological bent. And maybe it
governs what is redemptive in his conclusions on the
museum.

God has withdrawn from the world, abandoning it to
the violence and vanity of acts and works. Human history is nothing other than that of the animals or the
stars, a mixture of necessity and chance, both blind. Despite the cares with which the ego's narcissism wraps its
existence, the history of an individual life is likewise inconsistent: the ego, "a miserable little stack of secrets,"
according to the famous formula with a Pascalian accent.
I will say, laconically: every given is impugned *as such*. It
suffices that the given is *given* for it to be tarred by nullity. The giver having gone bankrupt, Malraux does not
receive, he takes. Conquests, the will, he repeats. And
just enough realism to metamorphose the said reality.
Metamorphose it, not "change the world." This difference establishes Malraux's relation to Marxism.

Therefore, there is first silence, nothingness. That doesn't
answer. But there is the question. That it remains with-

out answer does not give it the lie (*ne la dément pas*), on the contrary. There would be no way to understand that the world, the I, the we are left deserted were they not put to the question. Silence proceeds from the question. Herein lies the enigma: that the question of being and meaning can emerge out of dumb nothingness. That life is never dead enough not to let out the cry of abandonment. Malraux writes of Goya: "painting is not in his eyes the supreme value; its task is to cry aloud the anguish of man forsaken by God" ("Museum without Walls," in *Voices of Silence*, p. 99). Question, demand, anguish: the alert, in a word. All value, to pick up that Nietzschean word, is gathered into defying the inert, into what Malraux calls creation, and which is writing, the inscription of the cry.

Works of painting, sculpture, architecture, and literature are worth nothing as responses to nihilism, they are worth everything as questions asked of nothingness. Nothing insofar as existing objects, everything insofar as benumbed by the challenge of a monumention, of an alert that exceeds all givens and impugns all explanations. Explanations, like systems and conceptions, philosophies and intellectual labors, claim to have worth as responses to nothingness. They are lures, which smother and cloud over the cry. They make the abandonment forgotten, when it is only a matter of making sure not to forget that the world and life are absolutely forgetful. All the *meaning* the *mens* is capable of is that of unmasking non-being and non-sense, in making objects, human beings, and lives *inexist* through the writing of the scandal.

As a theme, the motif is obvious in the five novels. In Cambodia, Canton, Shanghai, Spain, and in between Berlin and Prague, the protagonists do nothing other than smash their will on the confines of nothingness. The will for what? For metamorphosis, that is, for signature. The adventurer, the political commissar, the militant anarchist or communist write the inert, the jungle, the masses, the Asian night, the fascist twilight in Europe, and always too, the internal chaos. And they sign, in vain. Even in *Days of Hope*, the protagonists' writing is imprisoned within a desperate story.

This carceral condition of writing is underscored in the essay on *La Jeunesse européenne* (European Youth) and in *The Temptation of the West.* And *The Walnut Trees of Altenburg* states that only books "hold their own against" prison, and especially those three books that were "written, the first by a former slave, Cervantes; the second by a former jailbird, Dostoievsky; the third by a former victim of the pillory, Daniel Defoe" (trans. A. W. Fielding [New York: Howard Fertig, 1989], pp. 90–91). Here is the jailbird's ideal library. Likewise, the imaginary museum would be the prisoner's album: visionary thought interned within the misery of life and defying the visible in the name of the possible. At the end of *The Voices of Silence*, we read: "The vast realm of art which is emerging out of the past for us is neither eternal nor extraneous to history; it bears the same relation to history as Michelangelo did to Signor Buonarroti, being at once involved in it and breaking free from it. Its past is not some age gone by, but a *possible*" (p. 635; translation modified).

It is said that works of art are imprisoned in the museum. On the contrary, they are incarcerated within reality, within cult or cultural objects; and the museum, by distancing them from the contingency of their occurrence, can write and deliver what there is of writing and of the cry within them. Monumention suspends the course of the deaf and blind world that casts the work, like every object, into the inert.

The museum does not arbitrarily transform the remainders of events into traces if it is true that its selection is guided by listening to the cry those remainders were smothering. The curator and the exhibit director lend an ear to the voices of silence, just as the analyst does to the voices of the unconscious.

You might object that such a responsibility is only exercised by art museums and does not obtain when the collection has the aim of reconstituting as faithfully as possible the landscape of an ethnicity or the tableau of an era. It is then necessary to gather and set out nearly all the documentary material with a view to rendering the object of this research intelligible. That's possible, but it is not certain that the understanding of an object is better served by an integral and rational exhibition of the documents than by a more allusive choice and disposition, that is, by a writing of the visit's space-time.

It will be conceded, however, that a museum of history, ethnology, or technology does not have the same obligations as an art museum. Just as the latter takes the imaginary, in Malraux's sense, as a model, so must the former bend to what one calls reality. Now, realist history, the cognition of how objects are transformed in chronological time, is in a sense the greatest enemy of the writing of the event, since it is, in principle, obligated to locate its motivation in the context, that is, in the event. It always encounters what Malraux ultimately calls the "autonomy" of the cry (Djidzek's autography) as an enigma: it is the fact of genius, historicism confesses. This is a way of saying that alertness does not belong to the "stream" of events and institutions, a stream according to which they follow upon each other and in which they are immersed, even if alertness emerges nowhere else but in the flow of evanescent conjunctures.

The imaginary museum is thus the writing of writing or the artistry of artistry. It monumentalizes the alertness that is present in the work and that does not pass away with its context. This inherent alert is already a monumention. The museum redoubles it, separates it, puts it in reserve, and hangs it up. It shelters it from what Malraux calls "satiating," from everything that turns works of art into the object of wild tranferences: prayers and sacrifices to powers, enjoyments, appetites, explanations, symbols. The museum secretly separates in the heart of the work between the given and the gesture that bears witness to the possible. And it compares this gesture to others, not out of concern for realist continuities (influences, contiguities, resurgences), but in order to make manifest the infinite variety of gestures, the thousand nuances of the cry. Fragmentations, montages, cut and paste: at a very young age, Malraux learns to work by comparing "manners." And this disjunctive manner is *his* own manner, already evident in the novels. It is also the manner of the imaginary museum, and the manner—strident to the point of madness—of his last essay, *L'Homme précaire et la littérature* (Precarious Man and Literature).

The imaginary museum can only be "modern." In effect, the civilization in which the museum appears must have lost all belief in order for it to be able to receive objects from every belief without judging them to be stupid, barbarous, and inaccessible like plants that are born, grow, and die (if we are to believe Spengler). Writing must have renounced every legitimation other than its autography for it to recognize, beyond the legitimacies expressed in works from other places and times, the ontological fact of autography in those works: creation, in Malraux's term. "For there is a fundamental value of modern art . . . : that immemorial will to create an autonomous world, a will which, *for the first time in history, has been reduced to itself alone*" (*The Voices of Silence*, p. 616; translation modified; emphasis added).

The resolute deception required by nihilism obligates this "reduction" of the will to itself alone by depriving the will of its transferential objects. "In ceasing to subordinate creative power to any supreme value, modern art has revealed the presence of that creative power throughout the whole history of art" (ibid., p. 616; translation modified). Within the temporality of art or of writing, the contemporary of Manet, the painter of nothing, is not "potboiler" conventionalist painting, it's

Giotto for the destruction of depth, it's the artist of Lascaux for *cut-off* contours.

In his first published text, *Des Origines de la poésie cubiste* (On the Origins of Cubist Poetry) (1920), Malraux gives special hommage to Max Jacob. What distinguishes a work of art, according to the latter, from any requested object, is its "situation" and its "style": "The style or will creates, that is, separates; the situation distances." The work *stands* by itself, as both daughter and mother of itself. It impugns every authority exerted on it, that of the supposed author as well as of the public's expectations. It unsubmits itself from the expression of the ego or a we, and from the representation of realities. It "has ceased to please in order to be. [It] is like a cubist painting," we read in one of Max Jacob's letters.

The terms of separation, style, creation, and will appear as recurrent motifs in *The Voices of Silence* and *The Metamorphosis of the Gods*. Reconnected or compared to cubist poetics and plastic art, they cease to speak the language of aestheticism, tragic humanism, or the heroism of revolt. They speak autography against a background of nihilism.

The imaginary museum is cubist, once again not because cubism was an important current of the avant-garde within the history of arts and literatures at the turn of the century. The museum is cubist because the cubism of Picasso and Braque exposed the excess of vision that is possible beyond every given view and that this excess, which is the essence of visual art, is precisely what the imaginary museum in turn sorts out from among works of art: art (in this case, writing) is what calls upon the possible, what is "wholly other" than the sensible, but within and through the sensible.

I have tried to do a little housecleaning in the museum by getting rid of the approximations and equivocations in Malraux's vocabulary, as well as his epic or preacherly eloquence. But what one accordingly sweeps away is never nothing. The difficulty in Malraux's opus is that of pursuing the nihilism further than is permitted by a secret desire of remission. As if the critique of metaphysics or of religion hadn't struck home. As was the case for Nietzsche with the thesis on the will, or with faith for Claudel (whom Malraux admired). I wouldn't say that this resurgent metaphysics is the speculative dialectics of a Hegel. A number of texts expressly oppose this.

But I don't think I'm the only one to sense, within his writings on art, the obscure design for salvation that governs them. Maurice Blanchot takes note of this suspicion in *L'Amitié*. It is as if, by entering into the museum or the library, writing whether visual or literary felt institutionally assured of escaping from nothingness. Of course, once they've entered the museum, the traces of writing that works of art are can undergo as many metamorphoses as are required by new comparisons. This is the way in which history and its contingency penetrate the holy place of monumention. They introduce new traces into it, they slip new gazes into it. The supernatural turns into the unreal, and the unreal into the timeless. But never into nothingness. Like at the Académie française, the signature is immortalized by its being established. It forgets that the threat of oblivion always remains. It forecloses its own lack of being. It fetishizes itself. In Malraux's opus, there is a fetishism of names that are signed. *Le Miroir des limbes* (Limbo's Mirror) is almost entirely built around "great" signatories of history. Compare Malraux with other writers of nothingness, Kafka, Camus, Blanchot, and you will see more clearly how the fetishization of the name throws an obstacle before the motif of autography. Without speaking of the labor Beckett's opus does on the signature.

A second, more common observation casts still more suspicion on the status of the museum in Malraux. One of the meanings of the word "imaginary" is to designate the object that supposedly answers a demand that is always a demand for love and survival. What if Malraux's museum, in the final analysis, were nothing more than a good transferential object?

In the context of the *pax occidentalis*, it is reasonable to think that there are no more subjects for destruction and ruin. But that's not where the threat lies. At the end of the General Introduction to *The Metamorphosis of the Gods*, Malraux concludes the following after listing off the millions of human beings who visit museums, interim exhibits, historic cities, and treasures: "People of all lands, hardly aware of what it is they have in common, seem to be asking of the art of all time to fill a void they dimly sense within them" (*The Metamorphosis of the Gods*, trans. Stuart Gilbert [London: Secker and Warburg, 1960], p. 34). But twenty-five years earlier, he judged it "rash to assume that the emotions the modern crowd expects from art are necessarily profound ones;

on the contrary, they are often superficial and puerile" (*The Voices of Silence*, p. 515).

The two observations are not incompatible. They may be conjugated within the frame of the following suspicion: that relentless frequenting of the museum is governed by the "superficial and puerile" need to install art—which is from that moment called "culture"—in the place of absent gods, and by the recurrence of the appetite to believe. Then, the secret and almost mute alert that is the *mens* inscribed into works of art remains unheard.

The work is ignored in its heterogeneity, it becomes that object of imaginary satiation that the culture industry produces. The *monumentum* turns into the establishment, even though—and because—nothing is established. And writing is forgotten as a cry of alert.

If this were the case, the museum would carry out a mortal menace on art. Artists would be tempted to work in order to enter it and to immortalize *their* signatures at little cost. It would suffice to please the curator or the exhibit director, to whom it would suffice to please the demands of the crowd. The *monumentum* erected against the inert would become the establishment of oblivion.

crypts

chapter 12

Unbeknownst

If we had time—but that's the whole point, we don't have the time (after a certain age, this is well known; whereas earlier, we believe we have time; to grow older is to learn that we will not have had the time; and Europe is old, face-liftings notwithstanding)—if we had time, we would seize the opportunity afforded by subjects like "The Politics of Forgetting" or "May '68: Twenty Years Later" to make a point by taking stock of where we are (*faire le point*). An illusory wish, and necessarily so. Points are marked out in space—in the middle of the ocean or in vast deserts—to which coordinate measurements are applied. But there are no points in time. We cannot even claim to be located in the immensity of time. Time discourages the attempt to "coordinate" and the hope of "locating ourselves."

In wanting to "mark out our point" (*faire le point*) we are already going astray. We are already forgetting what time is. Or rather, through the subterfuge of the spatial metaphor, time allows itself to be forgotten. Physicists have understood this, but not the rest of us humans.

It would not be a point, but on the contrary a universal proposition that we could make, one affirmed from every possible point: namely, that all politics is a politics of forgetting, and that nonforgetting (which is not memory) eludes politics.

I am not speaking of something that we could attribute to politics itself, of an intention to make forgotten. Intention has nothing at all to do with it. It's rather a question of "short-term memory," of that temporal disposition included in the rules governing a civil or citizenly community of whatever kind, and which requires that something in it be forgotten. What we could say is that what is forgotten, of course, is that this community remains intractable (*intraitable*) to the treatment of political unity; or again, that this treatment has in appearance to be renewed "from time to time," while in reality it has to be renewed all the time, perpetually. What cannot be treated, what is not manageable (*traitable*) once and for all, and what is forgotten by political treatment in its constitution of a "commonality" of humans by dint of their belonging to the same *polis*, is the very thing that is not shareable among them, what is not communicable or communal or common at all. Call it birth and/or death, or even singularity. On this, see Jean-Luc Nancy's *The Inoperative Community* (trans. Peter Connor, Lisa Garbus, Michael Holland, and Simona Sawhney [Minneapolis: University of Minnesota Press, 1991]).

Here, I do not wish to conjure up some kind of aggressiveness, death drive, or death struggle among humans that are whole, constituted, and organized into sects, parties, or movements. Nor even organized into individualities who rebel against any kind of association. It is the business of politics to make that sort of separation its business. Politics never ceases calling for union, for solidarity; and in the least bad of cases, it turns the manner of being together into the object of an open-ended negotiation, the object of a better-distributed justice or of a consultation that remains to be pursued. This daily fare of politics is not an easy matter. It is the art of Machiavelli. And ever since the authority of partitioning and sharing (*partage*) was denied "real presence" after and by the execution of Louis XVI, we know that the so-called democratic debate not only bears on possessions (economic, moral, intellectual) to be divided, on rights to be affirmed and taken into account in deliberation and distribution, but that the debate also, inclusively, bears on the authority that governs the debate and, sometimes, even on the very principle of the debate, at the constitutional level.

That is what was exposed in its horror when old Europe suffered its "crisis" during the era of totalitarianisms. Aside from that horror, there remains the striking fact, noted by Hannah Arendt and Franz Neumann,[1] that the totalitarian apparatus, constituted as a result of the elimination of debate and by the continuous elimination of

---

1. Hannah Arendt, "The Totalitarian System," in *Origins of Totalitarianism* (New York: Harcourt, Brace, 1951); Franz Neumann, *Behemoth: The Structure and Practices of National Socialism* (New York: Oxford University Press, 1942).

debate from political life by means of terror, reproduces within itself, in the anatomy and physiology of its national body politic, the illness that it claims to cure. Disorder within, an internal proliferation of decision-making authorities, war among inner-circle cliques: all this betrays the recurrence of the shameful sickness within what passes for health and betrays the "presence" of the unmanageable (*intraitable*), at the very time that the latter is hidden away by the delirium and arrogance of a unitary, totalitarian politics.

Betraying the unmanageable, these factors manifest it anew while reversing its meaning, and indeed by the very fact of reversing its meaning. Shiny, jackbooted rigidity is like the obverse of a poorly circumscribed thing that "inhabits" society without even being felt. With the horror resulting from this sanitizing operation, the phantasm of oneness and totality is sustained by the belief that this heterogeneous thing has, or is, a face (Medusa's face?), and that it would suffice to turn it around to get rid of it. And indeed, it is endowed with a face, with a name, a representation ("the jews,"[2] for example) wherein is invested everything that is supposed to be contrary to the distinctness—and inauspicious for the health—of the social body. But precisely, the thing has no more of a reverse side than it has a right side, it has no place, not having taken place and being "present" only outside representation: in death, in birth,

---

2. See *Heidegger and "the jews,"* trans. Andreas Michel and Mark S. Roberts (Minneapolis: University of Minnesota Press, 1990), p. 3, for an explanation of my use of quotation marks and lowercase for "the jews."

one's absolute and singular dependency, which prohibits any instantiated disposition of oneself from being unitary and total. I could just as well say "sexual difference," in the most radical sense of a heteronomy that does not belong to the space-time of representation. That is why it can hardly be felt in the "soul of the *polis*."

It is felt, in the sense that it is not heard or seen. It is not represented either by words or by "things" (images), as Freud used to say. Freud also designated its mode of "presence" by using the senseless expression: "unconscious affect." It has nothing to do with the imaginary nor, consequently—looking at the thing socially—with ideology.

I leave to Nicole Loraux, whose theses I am approaching here, the question of whether it is permissible to envision the thing socially.[3] In my opinion, there is no doubt about it, but I understand that historians resist the hypothesis that the *polis* has a soul, and that one must therefore disarm their defenses. No doubt there is *some soul* at stake in the polis, if by "soul" we mean the part of spirit that remains hostage to the thing, that remains susceptible to anguish, and defenseless. Historians, after all, are also trying to build a *polis*, and they strive, or lend themselves, to forgetting that affect.

What is essential to the unmanageable thing is that it absolutely must be gotten rid of. It can be approached

---

3. Nicole Loraux, "L'âme de la cité," *L'Ecrit du temps* 14/15 (1987), pp. 35–54.

only as the unbearable, the repulsive. Its way of attracting is to repulse. At least, that is what the mind recounts about it when it obeys the ancient call of the *logos* (the conceiving function) to corral, to determine, to expose, and to articulate everything—even the untimely thing—as an object. For, as far as the mind's clandestine passenger is concerned, we can and must suppose that it does not enter into the economic and dynamic game of attractions and repulsions, and that it is not waiting for us to concern ourselves with it or to "redeem" it by intelligence. It is what "occupies" the mind while disabling it. This occupation solicits a kind of paranoia. The "discontent of civilization," the sharp and vague feeling that the civilians are not civilized and that something is ill disposed toward civility, all this easily engenders the suspicion that plots are being hatched. Also easily engendered are trials, the denunciation of scapegoats, the exclusion of the *xenos*, the accusations made against opposing parties, slander, eristics. And the idea of revolution, too. *Polemos* is not the father of all things, he is the child of this relation of the mind to a thing that has no relation to the mind. And *Polemos* too is a way for the mind to forget it, to forget the *coïtus impossibilis* that engendered it and never stops engendering it.

If the thing is not manageable politically, it is because it is outside the chain. If we seek to link it onto the chain, which is the whole business of politics, it remains unlinked and only inspires yet more unleashing. Revolutions, all revolutions, are attempts to approach it, to make the community more faithful to what, unbeknownst to it, inhabits it; at the same time, revolutions attempt to regulate, to suppress, to efface the effects that the thing engenders. There is a fidelity and an infidelity in the fact of revolution. An attentiveness to what "is not working," a voice and an ear lent to a grave wrong done to the community, whatever that wrong may be called. Marx, for example, revealed its cause, or so he believed, in the exploitation of labor power, in the sacrifice of pure creative power that results from the capitalist organization of being together. I say "pure" creative power, because Marx endows it with an attribute that no mechanism of exchange possesses (be it chemical, physical, or human), namely, the property of expending or consuming *less* energy (less value) than it produces as it goes into action (into productive action, that is, as it goes to work). Thus, this power must be unleashed from the chains that bind it in the intrigue of the contract and on the stage of the market. It must be unbound from the *pseudon* (contract, work, average social time required) in which it is preferred, imagined, exposed, betrayed. Revolution, according to Marx, clearly means this fidelity to the non-enchained.

It seems to me that May '68 was marked by such a fidelity. From the outset, the unleashing expanded to culture. May '68 was faithful to the thing that would suffer from its being represented and directed toward the civil sector, the thing that would therefore be ill treated, not only in the factory or the office, but also at school, and throughout the institution of "culture" (which became manifest at that time and which today we encounter everywhere), and, of course, in political

life itself. In the streets of France, the thing was supposedly exposed live—at the cost, of course, of a thousand
ideologies of the most contradictory kind. But this very
incoherence in the representations can be chalked up to
a kind of fidelity, which it served to guarantee. The
question of political power was hardly asked, in the
final analysis. When, in late May and June, it did get
asked by the left, extreme or not, on the rostrum and at
work, when the political parties began once again to
bark up a storm, the thing fell silent, if indeed it had
ever spoken, or even heaved a sigh. The effects of the
unleashing persisted, but in the guise of traces. Like any
memory, although sometimes in the very name of fidelity, the function of these traces was always to help
forget the threat that everyone, whether in the movement or against it (always both at the same time, no
doubt), had experienced. One strives to become a realist, an activist, either stupidly or intelligently. By "intelligently" I mean with the Machiavellian intelligence
that is aware at least that politics cannot avoid betraying
the thing. In any case, realism requires amnesia.

Thus it is that the success of revolutions is necessarily their failure, and that their infidelity is produced out
of the very "exploit" or exploitation of their fidelity. On
the political "score card" (at once disastrous and illumi-
nating) that, unbeknownst to it, the century coming to
an end is mentally tallying up, a question arises: are
there other politics—other than revolutionary—that
would make it possible not to be unfaithful to the thing
that inhabits the *polis* unconsciously?

But how could such a goal be achieved by a politics, when politics is already devoted to the scene of representation from which the unpresentable presumably must be eliminated, unless politics is to risk losing the *polis*? The very manner of speaking about forgetting here, I realize, makes no political sense. Only a sense of melancholy. While giving up on revolution, we still cannot finish mourning for this fidelity, even though, and above all because, we know it to be impossible. Politics will never be anything but the art of the possible.

In this state of affairs, recourse to human rights brings slight consolation. Human rights define only the limits that public power ought not to cross. They can do no more than prohibit public power from unleashing the *polis*, in the way that all legal entities are limited. Human rights must be respected like a clear memory and a clear-sightedness, the memory of itself that the republic must conserve if it does not wish to fall into ruin. Human rights, then, are defensive. They are defense mechanisms against the nonlinked, and as a citizen, one has the duty to internalize them and to put them to work in public situations, to direct them to all others, oneself included. As such, human rights are one of the ways to forget: to forget that, in every mind and in the ensemble of minds that is the republican community, there is something that has no rights that needs to be affirmed, but that, beyond the just and the unjust, exceeds the mind of each and all. In the republican principle, humanity and its autonomy blur, under the guise of laws and rights, the traces of an immemorial independence.

"Resistance" can be used in two senses. Rights resist

the thing, and the thing resists rights. Clear memory resists the immemorial that threatens it, derails it, wears it
down like the clouds of matter that can slow the course
of photons approaching from far away. It is in this way
that our present relation to the idea of Enlightenment is
altered by the thickness of a night. Elie Wiesel's *Night*.
And you can't escape this aporia by adding memory to
the list of human rights. If one had to situate the respect
due the thing in the doctrine of justice, one would be
obliged to count it among the duties rather than among
the rights. It is the debt, par excellence. But, yet again,
the thing does not belong to a doctrine, it expects and
requires nothing from the mind, it exceeds all prescription—even all permission—of an institutional nature.
If, unbeknownst to it, the mind is indebted to the
thing, it is not because the thing has been contractually
instituted as the mind's creditor following a request for
a loan. The mind will have been dispossessed "before"
being able to certify or to act as a subject. It is con-
signed to the unending effort to repossess itself over and
against the thing, which means to forget it. This thing
will turn out always to have been the mind's childhood,
this enigma that the mind existed "before" existing.

The events of May '68—once shorn of their hodge-
podge of intentions, wills, strategies, and conciliatory
illusions—took on their luster, an intelligible luster,
really, from what they revealed of childhood. I do not
mean that the movement was motivated and carried
along by a collective infantile regression, nor even that
the majority of those swept up in it obviously were

young people. I mean that May '68 clearly showed a scrupulous fidelity to a state of dependency more immanent to the mind than its state of mind. This state of dependency was, I repeat, an unbearable one, and we were protesting against it without being able to name the cause (indeed unnameable). But at the same time, it was an admirable state that we insisted deserved homage, as if we could in that way get the civil community (the adult community) to recognize that, despite its ideals of autonomy and progress (or because of them), such a community could not avoid leaving a residue beyond its control, to which the community itself remained hostage, unbeknownst to it.

The return to order that all the political parties prescribed in different styles but with a single voice, from the extreme left to the right, was quite simply an urgent request to forget this childhood thing. The Marxisms, from the more radical Workers' Council movement to the less radical Maoism, had their part, a decisive part, in occulting what was being revealed—or rather what was showing itself. Each in its own way rendered the thing manageable once again by inscribing it within the register of political perspectives, including that of "splinter-group activism," the supreme nonsense, or countersense, with regard to the thing.

In the West at least, in the West of politics and metaphysics, any revelation is for the mind the event, perhaps, of a greater proximity to the forgotten-unforgettable thing, which leaves it disabled. The event of 1968, "les événements," as we have since called it in France, is remarkable for the anguish it taps. In the mind, childhood is not happiness and innocence but the state of dependency. Childhood itself seeks to rid itself of that state and to become "grown-up." It does not give evidence of its irresponsibility as a self-flattery, but as a complaint. May '68 sighed the lament of an incurable suffering, the suffering of not having been born free. This lament returned in an immense echo. Like a tragic chorus, adults lamented the lament of child heroes.

And yet, May '68 was not a tragedy; there was no denouement, no crime, and if blood was spilled, it was not the doing of the enraged children. They were not fulfilling a destiny inflicted on them by an oracle requiring their life's passion. Its representation as tragedy itself seemed, no less than politics, still too unfaithful to the thing. May '68 was not a revolution, because its actors were just young enough or old enough, just aware enough of the status of the *polis*, to know instinctively that today politics can in no way be tragedy. They knew that tragical-political terror is only an effect, and that horror (its true name) repeats the immemorial terror in which the mind has been dispossessed. They did everything they possibly could to avoid this repetition. They did not want, in their acts, to repeat the terror, born of the thing, but to invoke it through their gesture, as poets.

Since it was not revolutionary, the movement of May '68 was not destined to fall into unfaithfulness. Once the "demonstration" had shown that all politics is a politics of forgetting, it remained such as it was in our minds, serious and inconsistent, even as our minds forgot it. "Les événements" became *unheimliche*, both strange and familiar, like the thing to which they had borne witness. Their innumerable "effects" (school, sex, woman, family, work, etc.) came to be inscribed not as effects of '68, but rather as new initiatives in ordinary political and civil life. The West went back to its work of managing the unmanageable (*traitement de l'intraitable*).

chapter 13

The Intimacy of Terror

The contemporary world offers a picture of liberal, imperialist capitalism after its triumph over its last two challengers, fascism and communism: so Marxism would say, were it not defunct. A posthumous critique, for which the system has no concern. It is quite simply called the system. It does not permit peace, it guarantees security, by means of competition. It does not promise progress, it guarantees development, by the same means. It has no others. It arouses disparities, it solicits divergences, multiculturalism is agreeable to it but under the condition of an agreement concerning the rules of disagreement. This is what is called consensus. The intrinsic constitution of the system is not subject to radical upheaval, only to revision. Radicalism is becoming rare, as is every search for roots. In politics, alternation is the rule, while the alternative is excluded. Globally, the system functions according to the rules of a game with several players. These rules determine the elements that are allowed and the operations permitted for every domain. The object of the game is always to win. Within the framework of these rules, freedom of strategy is left entirely open. It is forbidden to kill one's adversary.

The system is continually revised by its integration of winning strategies in the various domains: you could say it constructs itself. Its complexification allows it to control and exploit "natural" or "human" energies that were previously dispersed. Health is a silence of the organs, said René Leriche, the surgeon of pain. The system silences noises; in any case, it keeps watch over them.

Two principles of legitimation clashed in the politics and warfare of Modernity: God and the Republic, Race and Universal Humanity, the Proletariat and the Citizen. This conflict for legitimacy, whether national or international, always took the form of civil and total war. Postmodern politics are managerial strategies, its wars, police actions. The latter do not have the aim of delegitimizing the adversary but of constraining it, according to the rules, to negotiate its integration into the system. If it has nothing to add to the game, being too poor, it can at least play out its indebtedness. As for the legitimacy of the system, it consists in its ability to self-construct. Out of this situation where right is based on fact, there result a few difficulties, in the administration of justice, for example, or in the aims of scholarly instruction. Finally, national frontiers are mere abstractions with regard to the needs of development.

In the face of these banal bits of evidence, "geo-noetics" appears obsolete. It belongs to a time when thought, *noesis*, believed it could be authorized by a land

and its name. German philosophy, the American dream, French thought, "English eyeglasses," as Rosa Luxemburg said. Or rather, it was the reverse: the "spirit" of a people became, for a time, the depository of and witness for a founding Idea: liberty in Athens, Philadelphia, or Paris; imperial peace in Rome, London; the saving race in Berlin or Tokyo. Each of these figures, be it bastardized, a racial Reich, or a republican empire, had a calling for which to fight.

Today, we say that the most appropriate system for development sought itself astride these conflicts between ideals housed under proper names. Each one was measured against its capacity to mobilize and organize the forces available in the demographic area whose name it proudly bore. In 1920, a little after the defeat of the German Empire, Ernst Jünger evaluated the Allied success in these cynically thermodynamic terms: a community of citizens who believe themselves free is better suited for a "total mobilization" than the hierarchical social body of Wilhelm II's subjects. This diagnostic was verified by the outcome of the Second World War and by that of the Cold War. The superiority of capitalist democracy is no longer at issue. Under the perfectly neutral name of system, it in truth emerges triumphant from several millennia passed in trying out all kinds of communitarian organizations. Human history was nothing more than a process of natural selection driven—precisely—by the competition between forms born by chance of the best performing one, the system itself. It's from this henceforth established fact that the world in its present state draws its prestige, or its authority, and it's to that fact that we (including the French . . .) give our consent: consensus proceeds from this self-evidence.

Need we be more specific? Respect for human rights, the duty of humanitarian aid, the right to intervene (as in Somalia), the status of immigrants and refugees, the protection of minority cultures, the right to work and to lodging, help for the sick and the old, respect for the individual in biological and medical experimentation, the right to schooling, respect for the individual in judicial inquiry and in conditions of incarceration, the right of women over their own bodies, the duty to give financial and technical assistance to the populations left destitute in the wake of the disappearance of the colonial empires and the Soviet Empire: these are, among others, problems to solve, questions to debate, sometimes with urgency. But always playing by the rules of the game, in consensus with the system.

Should this unanimity be called humanist? Yes, of course, if by that we understand that the system must show regard for the human beings of which it is made, but without neglecting, on the other hand, that the system requires the said human beings to bend to the needs of its development. For example, to be precise, they need to admit that, under current conditions, there is certainly no longer enough work for everyone in the production of goods and services. If there is humanism here, it must not, without risking imposture, be taken for the humanism of the Enlightenment. The latter gave itself the ideal aim of a community of equal and enlightened citizens deliberating with utter freedom about decisions to be taken concerning common affairs.

Humanism today is a pragmatism, less contractualist than utilitarian, where utility is calculated according to the supposed needs of individuals as well as those of the system. These needs are supposed, because within the system, games are always played with "partial information," as one said in the time of von Neumann and Rappoport: whatever one expects from opinion polls, statistics, and espionage, for the purposes of better locating one's adversary or partner (who are the same from now on), there remains an invincible margin of chance. (Unless I'm wrong, isn't the "veil of ignorance" John Rawls uses to dramatize his theory of justice simply the old concept of "incomplete information"?) But the system favors this uncertainty since it is not closed.

My point in recalling these banalities is not to signify that the world in which we live has nothing more to offer for thought and intervention. On the contrary, as we've seen, many things must be said and done, and must be proposed, precisely, within that margin of uncertainty that the system leaves to reflection. Who, among us, does not cooperate with this or that local, national, or international association, whose aim is to contribute to the solution of one or more of the— sometimes dramatic—difficulties I've named, or others I haven't named; and who does not publish, in one's own name, the reasons one has for opting toward this solution or that one and for helping to bring it about? We participate in debates, we enlist ourselves in combats no less than our ancestors, the Voltaires, the Deweys, the Zolas, or the Russells have done for two hundred years.

But they did it under wholly different auspices, and

for a wholly different price. Their combat invoked some ideal—the Common Folk, Freedom, the Individual, Humanity, in sum—not yet received within the system at that time; or if it was in principle received, it was in point of fact violated. In either case, they exposed themselves to censorship, to juridical proceedings, to prison, exile, to some kind of death finally, not of their body but of their speech. For their speech was insurrectional. As for us, whatever our intervention, we know before speaking or acting that it will be taken into account by the system as a possible contribution to its perfection. It's not that the system is totalitarian, as was long believed, still by Sartre, perhaps by Foucault, to their great disappointment (for no proceedings were ever made against them); on the contrary, its margin of uncertainty is quite open. One can't help but congratulate oneself on this latitude, but one must also measure the price that must be paid by thought and writing, which are our lot, for the attention that surrounds them.

That price was explicitly laid down in the program/article that Pierre Nora, one of the masters of the French school of history, published in the first issue of the journal *Le Débat*, which he had just founded in 1980. The moment had come, he declared in substance, to put an end to the disorder and the terror that reigned in French criticism and philosophy to the point of prohibiting all debate. Posing themselves as the inheritors of the artistic and literary avant-gardes, trying to outdo the incomprehensible poetics of Mallarmé or Artaud, reveling in the sibylline prose of the likes of Heidegger or Lacan,

Parisian writers and thinkers were forming groups who waged a war of words with each other, taking no care to make themselves understood by each other or by the public. Every sect pursued in schizophrenic fashion the illegible exercise of its talent. These irresponsible ones had ripped the cultural tissue to shreds, as the warfare between clans had in another time torn Gaul apart. It was time that some "Roman legion" brought order out of this anarchy and reconstituted, through debate, the order of the mind.

May Pierre Nora pardon me, I am too far from my hometown to cite the exact words of his text. I'm relying here on the impression of stupor that struck me in reading his text. We had an enemy, who showed himself, out in the open, in order to impose a *pax romana* on our domestic squabbles. He was advancing with the "heavy step of the Roman legions"—I remember that menacing metaphor. The new order did not take long in coming. The "new philosophers" in the workings of thought, the new subjectivity and trans-avantgardism in the visual arts, a poetics of procedures and genres, a genetics of texts, a sociology of cultural facts (considered to be merely the effects of forces at play in the social field), a history of mentalities, which in particular led to a treatment of the fact of revolution as a symptom: everything that called itself human science and positive reason advanced, with the noted "heavy step," to impose dialogue and argument on the aggressive and confused scriveners that we were. This spirit of seriousness had an assured advantage over us, which is that it had to exert no effort in attracting the favor of public opinion and of the media, which asked above all "to be able to know where they were" within the affairs of thought. The writings of the Roman Party were soon found on every dentist's coffee table, as Picabia used to say.

My stupor was as follows: Could the *Essays* of Montaigne become the object of a debate and would one be able to know where one was in reading them? Augustine's *Confessions*? *A Season in Hell*? But also Hegel's *Phenomenology*? And that of Husserl, or of Merleau-Ponty? Claude Simon's *Georgics, Doktor Faustus, The Castle*? What was there to debate, and how then to know where you were, in *Les Demoiselles d'Avignon*, in Delaunay's *Eiffel Tour*, Cage's *Mureau*, or Boulez's *Répons*, in Beethoven's thirteenth string quartet? Whether their material was language, timbre, or color, wasn't there some solitude, some retreat, some excess beyond all possible discourse, the silence of some terror, in the works of thought? And not out of capriciousness, fashion, or bravura, but in essence—if it was true, as Apollinaire said, that the work of art requires the artist to become inhuman. Is it possible without terror to bring something you don't understand to "signify" by means you don't control, since those means must be liberated from the ones tradition has controlled?

For works of art to be destined for entry in, or to have already entered, the World Museum, and to be catalogued in the Universal Library, and consequently filed away in the cultural stockpile, in memory, in rhetoric, which the system needs for differentiating itself, changes nothing pertaining to the fact that those works were never "produced" (what a word!) by the system, but only contextualized, being neither with it nor against it. They were born elsewhere, however, far from all communicational transparency: they are cultural objects, of course, and more or less accessible to the community, but irreducible to its usages or mentalities through the stunning power that we call their beauty and that resists the passage of time. This resistance and this opacity must be respected in the reception of works of art, even when one is trying to make commentary on them. Commenting is neither debating nor "finding where you are." It's rather about letting that residue follow itself out and allowing oneself to get lost in it: terror, once again.

I was not giving the works I cited by way of example with the intention of equating our poor essays with their greatness, but rather to recall that, in the face of what's called creation, the spirit of seriousness is not serious, nor are the claims of reason reasonable. True scholars are not unaware that this is how it is with scientific inventions: their appearance is no less wondrous than that of arts and letters; the state of knowledge in their time does not explain why they emerge; often they are resisted by that state of knowledge.

It does not follow that it suffices to be obscure in order to attain the measurelessness I am talking about. Nor to oppose a stony silence to the questions asked of a work of art in order to be its defender. Of those works I've cited, more than one was very civil and lent itself to discussion. That had no great importance, it did not hold the secret of the thing any more than another, but it may have liked to talk about it. Between the artist's studio or writer's desk—desperately lonely or rather deserted for the benefit of something unknown—and the armchair of conversation or roundtables, the gap remained and it remains unbridgeable.

Imagine Flaubert chatting about *Madame Bovary* with Bernard Pivot.[1] He would certainly have been able to do so, with all his knowing how to deal with received ideas. But how could Flaubert succeed in making the project of writing clear to our dear viewers, that overly subtle project that is less the project of writing about the distress of the petite-bourgeoisie than the misery of the model, received from the rhetoric of romanticism, by which it thinks it can express and soothe that distress? (And how, let us add in passing, could he make this clear to theorists of reception? Reception theory is precisely what Flaubert did in *The Dictionary of Received Ideas*, and in *Bouvard and Pécuchet*.)

I mention Flaubert, the Idiot in the family, because he was one of the first, like Baudelaire, to confront the stupidity of the system. Baudelaire writes in his *Notebooks*: "I cultivated my hysteria with joy and terror. Now, I've always got this vertigo, and today January 23, 1862, I felt before me *the breeze of imbecility flapping its wing*" (*Oeuvres complètes*, Pléiade edition, p. 1265). If you have to go to the point of becoming an imbecile, it's because "the world is about to end." We know this text, this "hors-d'oeuvre," as Baudelaire so appropriately

---

1. The host of a long-standing French television program, *Apostrophe*, in which writers were invited to discuss their works. —Trans.

calls it, which describes that outside-of-every-work that the world is in the process of becoming under the poet's horrified eyes. It's the stupid world of total exchange-ability, under the rule of money, the general equivalent for all commodities: goods, bodies, and souls. Our world (the system) is but the extension to language of the same routine of exchange: interlocution, interactive-ness, transparency, and debate, words are exchanged for words as use value is exchanged for use value. Poetic hysteria abruptly cuts off the circuit of repetitions. It confesses that it cultivates its retreat with joy and terror.

Where I hear repetition, Jürgen Habermas and Manfred Frank decipher a promise of liberty and equality. Isn't it true that messages are exchanged on the condition that they are comprehensible? And on the condition that you and I can occupy the positions of locutor and allocutor, one after the other. Richard Rorty goes so far as to maintain that this pragmatic condition is sufficient by itself to guarantee democratic solidarity, regardless of what is said or the manner in which it is said. Language may be "blank," like in Camus's *The Stranger*, but what matters is that it be addressed to someone else.

Human languages structurally confer on the locutor the capacity to speak to others. But capacity is not duty. It has not yet been proved that a willed silence constituted a fault. What is a crime is to impose that silence on another, who is then excluded from the inter-locutory community. Moreover, an even greater wrong is added to this injustice, since the one who is banished, being prohibited from speaking, has no means to appeal his/her banishment. Whether political, social, or cultural, the exercise of terror is as follows: to deprive the other of the ability to respond to that deprivation. Whatever else you may think, the death penalty however legalized always evokes this crime. But it could just as well be said that the child whose playmates say they will no longer play with him/her and refuse to talk about it is in truth the victim of a crime against humanity.

It is thus taken for granted that the human community rests upon the capacity for interlocution and upon the right to interlocution and that it's up to the republic to watch over this right and to teach that capacity. This thing—a banality, to speak truthfully—must be clearly stated in order to put an end to the accusations of irrationalism, obscurantism, terrorism, and sometimes fascism that have been leveled, here and there, against so-called French thought. It would be fastidious to refute in detail each one of these counts. The following ought to suffice: just as terror, and the abjection that is its doublet, must be excluded from the regime of the community, so must it be sustained and assumed, singularly, in writing as its condition.

That said, it is not forbidden to feel some unease on the subject of what founded, and perhaps still founds, the republican community itself. I know the system could care less and is trying to forget the Revolutionary Terror in France two centuries ago. Let's say, then, that the following reflections will have no importance.

In December 1792, during the trial of the king, held in his presence at the National Convention, Saint-Just turned to the right, on which side the Gironde was seated, and he declared: "This man must reign or die." The alternative excluded survival. Louis Capet could not enter into the republican community. As king, he held his authority from God. The only law the republic knows is that of liberty. When the head of Louis XVI was cut off in January 1793 in the Place de la Révolution, God was the one whose word was cut off. The republic, and hence interlocution, can only be founded upon a deicide; it begins with the nihilist assertion that there is no Other. Are these the beginnings of an orphaned humanity? That's not what Saint-Just understands. Nothing is more suspicious than an orphan, who incarnates metaphysical melancholia, whose thoughts keep alive the vanished father and mother. It is necessary that the mourning be completed. "Happiness," Saint-Just decides, "is a novel idea in Europe." Happiness, the forgetting of the murder, is a republican duty. Just one more effort . . .

While waiting for this terrible civic paradise, melancholics must be held in suspicion. This man who must either reign or die is the king, but every man must both reign as liberty and die as submission. Every motivation other than the fulfillment of the law of liberty is subject to suspicion: passions, interests, everything that lends itself to tyranny in the soul of the empirical people. Saint-Just's alternative thus draws a line between democracy, which is tyranny, Kant says, and a holy republic.

But where do you draw the edge of this line? Liberty, first of all, is an idea of reason, which is never unequivocally incarnated in experience. There is never any assurance that a given decree, taken in the name of reason, does not conceal unavowable motivations. Can one ever be sufficiently liberated of these, and how could you know it? Everyone, starting with Robespierre, is suspicious to him- or herself. Terror is exerted intimately.

And then, if liberty is what speaks the law, what can the law be, except: be free? Liberty is pure beginning. It is unaware of what was before its action, and thus too of the traces left by its previous actions. What can it institute? It cannot avoid dreading its works, on the same level as everything that precedes its present action, the entire ancien régime of the soul. Intimate Terror exerts itself without respite.

Do we need to recall these well-known things? Obviously, they must be recalled for the benefit of our adversaries. Their interest in consensus is surely not wholly republican in nature; it's also in the interest of the system, as I've said, in the interest of its calculations, which Baudelaire called Prostitution. And even if we give credit to their virtue, we beg them to remember the crime of which she is the child. The horizon of universal intelligibility to which they appeal has been detached by a bloody stroke. The price of the deicide cannot be measured, the debt of reparation will never be acquitted by some reasonable exchange on the subject, because that very exchange, its liberty and its right, are due to the crime.

The Terror is not just the historical event we know. Its gesture of interruption is repeated every time the republic legislates, every time the citizen speaks up. Liberty is supposed to be what pronounces the law, for all and for each, but it can never be sure that it is not corrupted by some utilitarian end. The era of suspicion is not ready to come to a close. Did Saint-Just know that the Terror would be the lot of a world dedicated to liberty? That brother would not cease to contest the authority of brother, that every tribunal could be impugned, that, for two centuries, Europe and the world would make war to decide how the law is incarnated and what it says? Politics became modern tragedy, Napoleon said. That's over now, and in consensus, we celebrate the disappearance of those quarrels of investiture.

That does not change the persistence of the torment, for "sensitive souls," of not being what one is, of being another and of not being that other, of having to answer to that other and for that other, who asks nothing definite. Augustine was the first, along with Paul, to reveal that inner split between the ego and the Other, who within the ego is deeper than the ego. Deeper insofar as the ego cannot comprehend the Other. Yet, Augustine still had faith that this Other, the God of love, wished only the good.

After the deicide, God did not succumb. Baudelaire writes: "God is the only being who does not even need to exist in order to reign." He reigns therefore, but his decrees, if there even are any, are incomprehensible. Even his law is suspect. How can we decide that what the Other inspires in us is not due to Satan? Evil is not the opposite of Good, it is the indecidability between Good and Evil. Just as corruption can pass for a virtue, Satan can pass for God. Bernanos said that faith today is to believe in Satan. But this is still to believe that the scandal will be pardoned. Now, the law of liberty, without permitted faith, has no power to keep this promise. Consensus is not to redeem the crime, it is to forget it. We are asked to help resolve the injustices that abound in the world. We do it. But the anguish of which I speak is of another temper than that of civic concerns. It resists the republic and the system, it is older than them, it protects and flees at the same time the inhuman stranger within us, "joy and terror," says Baudelaire.

If works of art are still possible, if the system is not what alone produces them and addresses them to itself, if therefore literature, art, and thought are not dead, it is because they hysterically cultivate this relation with what is irrelevant. Baudelaire says hysteria because this relation must inscribe itself—this is what writing means—and because it must trace itself in the matter of bodies, colors, sounds, in words too, that overabundant matter. Not in order to have a dialogue with these matters and for them to "speak" clearly (there is no need of writing for that), but to give them back to *their* silence, which makes so much noise in the human body, to expose them to their potentiality and to obtain from them the gesture of a poem.

Jean Paulhan, in *Les Fleurs de Tarbes* (The Flowers of Tarbes), subtitled *La Terreur dans les Lettres* (Terrorism in Literature), expressed his astonishment that the criticism of his time (this was the time of the Occupation, and Paulhan was occupied in working with a network of resistance—a lovely expression) kept on deploring the place given to the matter of language in writings of literature. They are only words, this criticism repeated, believing, along with Bergson, that language is merely the dead discards living thought leaves after itself. And so it is that Pierre Nora and many others enjoin us to be legible and communicable, to be consensual, in a word.

But if it's a question of writing, painting, or composing, what does one encounter right off the bat? Words, sounds, colors, not in a raw state, of course, but already organized by the rhetorics we have inherited, and also predisposed by our temperament in what Barthes after Buffon called a style: a history, a nature. And writing is the labor that aims to silence that learned or spontaneous eloquence. Here, terror exerts itself, to impose silence, and with regard to what is closest to us, to cut off the most familiar repetitions and expressions. By the same stroke, as with the law of liberty, a follow-up terror is set up, subjugating the previous terror for not knowing what it is that is desired in those mute and noisy matters.

The intellectual, once upon a time, was a happy writer or artist: his/her works, though obtained under the conditions we've described, had in themselves the power to call civil or political society back to its ideal destination. Intellectuals today do not need to be exposed to the trials of writing. They are called upon by the system to make public proclamations, for the sole reason that they know a little better than others how *to make use* of language to restate the urgency of consensus. The terror of which I speak comes down to this, that if one writes, it is forbidden to make use of language, which is the Other. One can, one must, do the intellectual thing on the speaker's platform. But in front of the canvas or the page, consensus is null and void.

chapter 14

Music, Mutic

It is a grave and common error to impose a classification by periods or schools on works of art. In reality, you're only classifying cultural products, which belong in effect to observable phenomena of historical reality, like political events, demographical mutations, and economic changes. But what there is that is art in works of art is independent of these contexts, even if art shows itself only within those contexts and on their occasion. The art of the work of art is always a gesture of space-time-matter, the art of the musical score, a gesture of space-time-sound.

This gesture is not the author's doing. The work of the author is to let the sound make a gesture that seems to surpass the audible and to consign its trace in the space-time-sound that determines the field of audibility. This gesture is no less emotionally powerful in No music than in a Schumann lied. The light in a fresco by Piero della Francesca is no less "invisible" than that found in a watercolor by Cézanne. Gestures, which are neither contents nor forms but the absolutely emotive power of the work, make no progress in the course of history. There is no history of art as gesture, only as cultural product. The power to affect sensibility beyond what it can sense does not belong to chronological time. Only what is called the "function" of art, the gesture's trace recollected within human communities, is what is transformed, and what may be periodized.

Music struggles, it *labors* in the strong sense of the word, that used by obstetrics and psychoanalysis, to leave a trace or make a sign, within the audible, of a sonorous gesture that goes beyond the audible. Such is the paradoxical idea, philosophical because it is paradoxical, that we need to explore. A twin paradox: a sonorous matter, first of all, which is not heard since it surpasses the audible, and which is nonetheless, if I may say so, *already* a sound. And then a gesture in and of this matter, and hence also in and of the space-time it deploys by this very gesture, a gesture that is not the doing, or not simply the doing, of a conscious subject, namely, the composer. Like the woman or the analysand *in labor*, the composer lets a passageway be opened through which something can happen that has *not yet* happened, a child, one's past, in this case a musical phrase, and that is nonetheless *already* potential human life, possible memory or eventual sonority. The conscious subject works on itself, with and against itself, in order to be accessible to the eventuality. The musical gesture strikes the ear, thus prepared for being unprepared, like an event. Not because it emerges unexpectedly, since on the contrary, it will have been awaited and violently wished for. But it is an event insofar as the subject giving issue to it did not and does not know *what* this event is, what it consists in, as one says. The composer does not control it.

Here, a correction is needed for what might seem an overly romantic way of raising the question. A correction that bears, this time, on the question of language rather than that of the subject. Whatever cares are taken by the composer for making inoperative his/her expectation and the hoped-for phrase, whatever the means of the work of reception by which the composer prepares the appearance of this phrase (to cite only two great contemporaries, Cage and Boulez: be it by the art of disconnecting timbres and letting them sound brashly, or by that of multiplying the constraints on how they are put into phrases so as to give birth, as if by a forceps, to the sonorous matter of the gesture not spontaneously given by the phrasing), sonorous *forms* result in any case from either "technique," just as they do from every inoperant procedure. The opus coming forth from this labor is audible, and the audible is heard because it is formed or can be formed in a language of sounds. The musical masterpiece cannot remain unknown to the ear. To open up a passageway for the sonorous gesture is necessarily to inscribe something of it in a language that speaks to the hearing, that affects auditory thought. The gesture may be an enigma, but its actualization within a human body sensitive to sounds does not signify the mystery of an incarnation.

And yet, if we are content to decipher and recognize these forms, to describe "how it's done"—surely a useful and necessary task—we treat the opus as a finished object, as a given that is just there. We don't attain, we don't even reach what is at stake in musical pieces that merit the name of opuses, namely, the enigma of letting appear, of letting be heard an inaudible and latent sonorous gesture.

It is advisable to yield to the principle that the forms of the made (heard) opus are the depository or archive, in the language of sounds, of a sonorous event that I call, for lack of anything better, the gesture, which by its very principle thwarts that language because it cannot be heard directly within it. What is audible in the opus is musical only inasmuch as it evokes the inaudible.

In extrapolating this principle, one is tempted to conclude that there is therefore sound both hither and beyond the languages of sound, of sound without language, of sonorous matter without form. And that the musical work takes its flight or draws its resources from a matter that is, of course, sonorous, but ultra- or infra-sonorous. The implication seems suspect, a metaphysical proposition, and pretty hazy. The idea of such an element may have a certain poetic value; it's not clear that the philosopher can grant it any credit whatsoever.

It is not unprecedented, however, for philosophy to go to poetry school and to profit from it. Especially when it is a question of approaching the enigma of artistic beauty, where conceptual discourse soon reaches its limit. It is good for thought, when it takes music as an object, to lend an ear to literature. The enigma of literature is certainly not foreign to the paradox of music, although the element by which the gesture literature tries to capture in the work comes into being as writing is surely utterly other than sonorous matter.

I'm going, for a moment, then, to impute the worry the philosopher feels concerning the enigmatic matter of sound to a very strange motive. It's the one sketched out, in a few pages, by one of the *Petits Traités* signed by Pascal Quignard: number twenty, titled "Language" (volume IV). Under such qualifications as "language beneath languages," of "sonorous depth," "sonorous horizon," and even "sonorous scent," I believe I hear something of the element I'm dreaming about. The text, in truth, doesn't deal with kinds of music, but with languages. But spoken languages, in such a way that the case permits analogy since, you understand, it is a question of sonority. Quignard takes care, and I will do as he does, not to hold forth on the origin of languages or music, and still less on how the origin of the one is to be found in the other. The question is not even that of a voice off, but of a *whisper off*.

Here is the short passage I take from the treatise "Language" (*Petits Traités* [Paris: Maeght, 1990], vol. IV, pp. 22–27):

"As different as people, civilizations, ages, languages and works of art may be, it sometimes seems, to the point of hallucination, that there arises from them the appearance of a terrified, general lament, which always seems to be naked and new, like a sonorous depth that makes you crazy. A language beneath languages, which is the sound of a fragment of collective fear, which everyone emits undoubtedly in one's own fashion, and to a greater or a lesser extent, but which always wanders from lip to lip, along the almost sexual and forever bared protrusion of faces, over the course of millennia. A perhaps elementary terror that human beings holding pebbles in their mouths have muttered for whole eras, which is also the very childhood in which it is renewed, and which gathers us together. This sound that moans, rhythmically, then arhythmically, then rhythmically again, this pleasure in lament is the true sheep-bell of 'the flocks who speak a language.' Languages cannot turn back on themselves, or turn around to show the truth about languages. It seems that this sound imprinted with fright that organizes us into groups, that bewails a dead father, that endlessly associates us into familial or societal forms, unites us without its enjoining anything other than its force. The lamentations of Baroque musicians in a chorus, in the darkness of a dead god. The sound of murder. C. M. Bowra was astounded that among the primitive chants transcribed by ethnologists you could count only hunting songs, a few about war, never any about love. To speak the truth, we would have to love ourselves a little bit in order to bear any esteem at all for beings who resemble us. We only resemble our prey. And our resemblance is made only in their image. It has happened rarely that we prefer ourselves above the tall and vertiginous chain of beings willingly listed by myths. It does not seem that there have been many beings that the gods have created upon a model other than their images. Certain stones more symmetrical and impassible than others—what if we associate viruses with these? Whom do we resemble?

"There is a great scroll—below the white froth—of similarities that scare us every time we become conscious of them. We all desire to be so singular at the same time that we make collections to the point of disgust.

"There is a sonorous horizon behind the backdrop of places. Bits of sounds of a fear that exploded long ago like the universe and that is hailed upon by depression, that is shackled by pleasure, that takes flight in suffering. Sounds whose recognition is more precisely an unending discovery, often tardy, which doesn't free us from itself. In this knowledge, we often interrupt ourselves with the belief in our originality. This discovery, if it leaves us in the desert, does not remove all worry. For lack of being able to find the original of anything, it does not properly speaking urge us in the direction of others. It dooms us to a solidarity from which we can never escape but to which suddenly we begin to consent too quickly, no matter how inevitable it may be. The perception of those fleeting shadows that suddenly pass over the faces of men and women coming toward us and that are an avowal of their sadness and mortality in truth gives us intense satisfaction. *At the end of these considerations*—however little we may have the courage to humiliate one after the other the illusions that lead us to believe we are essentially ourselves—*we no longer know solitude.* This sentiment is highly infectious. Solitude, though it strangles the solitary one in suffering, is a jewel no fortune is able to buy. And like darkness, it nears silence. All the languages of the world seem secondary with regard to this lament of hunger, distress, loneliness, death, danger. Just like beasts that like to rub themselves in their own stink, languages that are pronounced love the mass of voices. All the languages of the world, no matter how potent or skillful, do not cover over this 'sonorous scent' of the species. They have never covered it over and they never will."

Being a bit of a sophomoric schoolboy, I'm attempting to separate out of these lines some characteristics proper to the element of sound, the sound matter, whose gestures are inscribed by music and which gives its emotional power to the opus.

First of all, the sonorous appearance of this "language beneath languages" is available only to the hallucinated ear. At a level below languages, works, institutions, always lying latent beneath the audible but never covered over by it, this breath does not speak, it moans, it mutters. It has no history, it's a lament "that appears always naked and new," that has nothing to tell. It appears invincible to articulation, implicitly understood and prostrate even in the discourse of forms. It wanders over lips, its swells "the almost sexual and ever bared protrusion of faces," it rests ensconced in the thrust of voices stacking themselves one before the other in their millenary commerce.

Now, and this is the second, and very paradoxical, trait: though inaudible, this breath still makes a sound. It sounds deafly, Quignard explains, like "a terrified lament. . . . A lament of hunger, distress, loneliness, death, danger." The element of sound is the unheard exhalation of fright. The breath is a wind, a *flatus*, of terror: one is going to be no more. This wind is *deaf*, we are deaf to it. Maybe we *cannot* hear it. But it is not *mute*. Or else, it is mute in the sense of the old root *mu-*, *mut*. The terror lows, bellows, murmurs, it rustles its closed lips. "A mouth relay," Quignard writes later, "which puts exactly 'nothing' between your teeth." Nothingness doesn't let itself be articulated, you can't bite it. A toothless cavity, a flabby muzzle, is the torpid instrument by which nothingness whispers its horror, sounding a continuous bass. A night of sound rather than a shadowy mouth. No matter how clear the phrases of the clearest music might be, they bellow forth fright in secret.

Quignard underscores a third characteristic. The distress exhaled in this breath is common to the animal kingdom. It organizes people "into groups," he writes, like "beasts that like to rub themselves in their own stink." It's a sonorous scent of the flock. Dread is mutic, henceforth, inasmuch as it is not addressed and remains unaware of the other and the self. It inhabits their commerce but as a fraud. It disavows persons, pronouns and nouns, questions and answers, responsibilities. It prohibits us from "the belief in our originality." Barefaced distress crushes the singular below "the great scroll of similarities," it urges a panicked solidarity. The breath death exhales "endlessly associates us into familial or societal forms . . . without its enjoining anything other than its force."

Quignard adds: "We all desire to be so singular at the same time that we make collections to the point of disgust." The bestial lament is a *sensus communis* not of taste (*goût*), but of disgust (*dégoût*), a stinking breath constrained by an unmitigated horror. What lives is aggregated to what lives, all of a mass, by the stuffy smell of perdition. Life laments its precariousness in an ever forgotten, anonymous death rattle. I maintain that music gets its beauties and emotions from the evocation of this condition of abandonment that is loud and mute, horrified, moist with a promiscuity without alterity.

As for the sonorous element, the bellowing, it maintains itself, it will have been maintained by itself close to all, having come from the threatening void.

Such is, in summary, what Pascal Quignard imagines in the form of a "language beneath languages" and which I hijack in the name of a mutic beneath music. It is not said that music *would express* or *translate* a phobia among the living for whatever evokes their death. The terms of expression and translation are inappropriate. The breath of fright makes an unheard sound while the strings vibrate, and the cases and tubes resound. The more or less regulated sounds obtained by the clash of bodies (including the organs of human and animal bodies) are not the arrangements of a more fundamental music. Lamentation breathes forth without striking a blow, it does not echo like a vibration that has just struck an obstacle. Having no teeth, it has neither vocal chords nor phonatory cavity. It is not a music, be it an originary one, for lack of articulation. It is not audible since it doesn't resound. It doesn't resound because it results from no percussion. It's a *flatus,* a sub-flatus, from which our *breath* comes, an empty wind. It passes and does not pass, since it never stops passing through all the obstacles that engender the audible.

This breath is affect. Not an affect among others, or a modality of affection—angry, fearful, happy, languid—but affection. Affection is what animals do. Aristotle wrote: they feel, they are inhabited by *pathemata*. Animality is pathic. To be affectable is to be possible. Passibility is precariousness. One is not, one depends, one depends in order to be. A master shakes your hand, and grabs you, lets you go, and holds you back. He reminds you that you are not. It puts you out of breath. Life loses its breath, gives it up, gets it back, a disconcerting rhythm. Quignard writes: "This sound that moans, rhythmically, then arhythmically, then rhythmically again, this pleasure in lament." And he adds: "Bits of sounds of a fear that exploded long ago like the universe and that is *hailed* upon by depression, that is *shackled* by pleasure, that *takes flight* in suffering." A black night upon the desert, the hallucinated ear believes it grasps the breath of nothing, which is naked affection. Affective rhythms and nuances, pleasure, suffering, depression, modalize the sound of silence after the fact.

To modalize affects is already to put this noise to music, to make affection speak in shapes. The black lament that annihilation breathes forth persists in phrases and below them. (It doesn't make exchangeable phrases. It makes them rub each other, organize into groups, bellow.) Pleasure, the pleasure of this dread: as long as you moan, you're not dead.

Moaning has no tone. All tones are good for moaning. Breath is atonal. The art of tones, *Tonkunst,* opens up initially to any lament at all, and then modulates it. Music cannot make the breath heard, it cannot imitate it, since nothing audible can resemble it, it is constrained to phrase pathos, to nuance it, to cut it up into pitches, measures, loudness. The breath passes and does not pass. Affection, which is distress, remains immobile. Out of this duration without consequence music makes time that comes, that goes, starts up again, falls apart, is rhythmed into dead time and strong time, that tells itself like a passionate story. The art of tones cuts up the lament, defers its disastrous continuity, puts its sonorous fragments together, places them end to end.

Isn't this very active labor due to the power, and the competence, of articulated language, of discourse? This is a question we will not answer here. For lack of time, but also because it is badly framed.

A sound, an isolable tone, an island risen up out of pathos makes itself heard. With the appearance of the audible sound, a promise is made. This sound promises that there will be other sounds. Hence that there will still be something rather than nothing. The terror of being annihilated never ends, always inaudible since continuous, inarticulated, addressed to no one. Music labors to give birth to what is audible in the inaudible breath. It strives to put it into phrases. Thus does it betray it, by giving it form, and ignore it. But also, it promises. Every sonorous phrase, even the simplest, announces that there will be another phrase, that it is not yet over, that the end of phrases is not to come to an end, that in nothingness, music will echo itself. Every phrase asks to be honored by a phrase. The honor so rendered is sufficient to prevent the beast from floundering in fright and from being suffocated by the scent of sound.

Music is a hymn to glory and to the future of what is, in its distinction as entity and thanks to its infinite determinability, even while it keeps within itself, unheard, the echo of a stupidity subjected to the wind of non-being, that is, of being.

The phrase goes out toward you and asks you for a phrase. You formulate my demand by linking onto that phrase. In music, this is called *répons, responsaria, response* from as far back as Gesualdo up through Boulez. *Response* is not to answer, but to address and carry forward. From one response to the other, millennia are spent articulating, adjusting, and addressing the prostrate bellowing of melancholia.

A community is born, polyphonic even in plainsong, enchanted by sonorous apparitions even within the war of counterpoint. The community forgets the anonymous horde moaning with the terror of no longer being. The community, however, does not efface the horde. Even within *Don Giovanni*'s air of freedom, no less than in a Bach cantata or the adagio con motto of Schubert's Quintet for Strings, despair is implicitly understood. Even in *Children's Corner*, even in *Véritables Préludes flasques (pour un chien)*, even in the ritornello of *A Green Mouse*.

That being is lacking and does not lack lacking makes for a panic rumor. Despite itself, this rumor of non-being gives music the immaterial matter of apparitions, of gestures, that are transformed into phrased appearances.

From this, could one say that there is sound and pathos before there is music? But this sonorous depth is suspected only through the tonalities and passions of music. The unheard breath is implicitly understood only within and through the listening of musical language. The body must chant and enchant itself to give access to the delirium of the disenchanted body, to hallucinate within itself another body, one that is mute and doesn't stop toning down. Without music, how can an inaudible wailing be implicitly understood, how could it be imagined? It is as silent as the music of the spheres. They have no language and don't hear their own music. They wail on account of their being cast into the void. The wailing of the cosmos is mute. Only percussion, beat, and discontinuity make it sing, and allow for its terrible silence to be evoked after the fact.

A few lessons are easy to draw from this reverie on the shadows of sound.

There is a sonorous matter that is not what the musician calls the material. The latter is understood as the timbre of the sound. Matter is not heard, it is the sorrow of being affected. This sorrow wails; inarticulate, it asks nothing. Affection is the threat of being abandoned and lost. The breath of the lament, which is sonorous matter, clandestinely inhabits the audible material, the timbre.

Matter is the unproffered sound that passes into

the body upon receiving the blow of its loss. You might say it is the sound death makes in the living body. Or, again: the unheard sound that Being makes in the entity. Passibility or sensitivity opens up the body to trial. The latter is not an experience, but an affliction. Something that is not the body comes down on it. Before and within every reaction, this thing sounds its defeat within it, which it does not hear. It is beaten, that is, afflicted. The murmur of this offense is inaudible. Only the reaction, the musical putting into form gives body, opens up to something strange. But this is nothing, it is the nothing which *estranges* the affected body and breathes the terror of being abandoned into it.

The same goes for visual as for sonorous matter. The body is passible because it has doors and they are open. The same news enters through all these doors, always the same news—that it is not what it is, that it is nothing without affection, which nonetheless announces that it is nothing. What enters through the blazon of the body, sensations, *aisthesis*, is not just the form of an object, it's the anguish of being full of holes. And so it is for color. Color is the body penetrable by the visible, and it is then itself not visible without shapes and names. It is the suffering of a body visually bewildered. Painting articulates, modalizes, and makes seen the visual scent that is color. Color matter announces to the eyes that they are subject to something that is not them, and that they cannot itself see, since they can see thanks only to it.

Chromatically, this thing is nothing; within the body, it is its visual estrangement. Just as there is a mutism of sonorous matter, so is visual matter blind. You don't hear the terror of nothingness as a breath, and you don't see it as a light. The gaze is a return, a remedy and a reaction to the distress of that blindness. Just as the music of the spheres is an inaudible bellowing, so the colors of the universe that are said to shimmer offend the body with a mass of invisible vibrations, a neutral mass Paul Klee imagined to be gray. Gray is the uncolored color of the terror the eyes have of being lost, like moaning is the unsonorous sound for the ear.

Differences between the fine arts proceed from differences between these matters, that is, from the various ways, all contingent, the body has of being threatened by nullity, of being anesthetized: deaf, color-blind, bedridden, etc. Aesthetics is phobic, it *arises* from anesthesia, belonging to it, recovering from it. You sing *for* not hearing, you paint *for* not seeing, you dance *for* being paralyzed. In each of these arts, the tiniest phrase is equivalent to a remission from pain. By "*for* not seeing," "you paint *for* not seeing," I mean the following: suffocating gray is the element whose gesture is awaited by painting; painting inscribes this gesture in visible colors; it forgets the terror, which nonetheless motivates it.

Quignard writes: "a depth of sound that drives you crazy." We say: crazed with terror, paralyzed with terror, gray with terror, mute with terror. The supposition of this folly is itself mad, a kind of speculative hallucination. But it may be necessary to pay the price of this delirium in order to approach the idea of an art gesture.

If the work is art, it's because it bears witness to

something in excess of what the body can sense, of what is sensible as circumscribed by the (biological, cultural) institutions of the body. What the speculation of folly tells us is that this excess is *already* at the very origins of sensation, right in its matter and perhaps nowhere else. Sensation is not only the reception of useful contextual information, it is also in its immediacy the reminder of a threat. The body doesn't belong to you, it is sensible only insofar as it is exposed to the other thing, deprived of its self-distinction, in danger of annihilation. It is sensible only as lamentable.

The transcendence—whether beautiful or sublime it matters little, the difference not being discernible in relation to the work—of the work of art is found right there in the evocation of this precariousness forever enveloped in sensation. Transcendence depends on the immanence of an affliction.

The gesture of music labors to let the inaudible lament come forth to what is audible. But in order to do that, music must give form to the lament. Thus, it can never really attain it. It covers it. This labor in vain can, however, suffice to evoke, within the language of music, the breath of fright. The bellowing is obstinate, permanent, like the urgency of not dying. That's why the testimony the work of art can bring forth, be it always suspect, that testimony we call its beauty or sublimeness, is not perishable either. It transits through historical conjunctures, as the breath of being downbeat glides across the beats that segment sonorous space and give music its materials.

chapter 15

Anima Minima

When ideals turn out to fail as objects of belief and models of legitimation, the demands of cathexis are not disarmed, they take as their object the manner of representing those ideals. Kant called this manner the *modus aestheticus* of thought. Aesthetics is the mode taken by a civilization that has been deserted by its ideals. It cultivates the pleasure of representing them. And so it calls itself culture.

The ideals of Western civilization issuing from the ancient, Christian, and modern traditions are bankrupt. The cause of the bankruptcy is not in what is called historical, social, political, or techno-scientific reality. The recurrent crises, or rather, the permanent crisis, the West talks about in its becoming proceed from an essential disposition. The West is that civilization that questions its essence as civilization. The singularity of Western civilization resides in this questioning, which in return endows it with a universal import—or so it claims.

With a repeated gesture, the West arms itself with ideals, calls them into question, and rejects them. This gesture is not the sole doing of philosophy, that is, of the Greek tradition. There is no less doubt or potential nihilism in Christian mystery or in the physics and metaphysics of classical modernity. Whatever the name given to it by tradition, the power of the negative in that name raises its pretension to universality and promises to realize and comprehend every possible experience. Absolute knowledge requires a full-blown nihilism.

Aesthetics claims its actuality (being present, in action) because the West actualizes its nihilism by contemplating the ruined ideals it leaves behind it with a melancholic satisfaction. Aesthetics is new because nihilism is old. The West knows that civilizations are mortal. But knowing this suffices to make it immortal. It makes itself the world's museum. It thereby ceases to be a civilization. It becomes a culture.

We have many words to gloss the aestheticization inherent to culture: staging, spectacularization, mediatization, simulation, hegemony of artifacts, generalized mimesis, hedonism, narcissism, self-referentialism, auto-affection, auto-construction, and others. They all speak to the loss of objects and the ascendancy of the imaginary over reality. You can take an inventory of this gentle deception in every field of activity and thought: the "human sciences" can speak forever on this subject. Let me cite haphazardly: the extinction of rural societies, the ecological stockpiling of nature, the tele-war in the Gulf, monetary metaspeculation, science as artistic invention, the disavowal of politics, all the "liberations" of women, of children, of minorities, of sexualities. Culture consists in dissipating what there is of destiny, sorrow, and finitude in the existence of individual or collective bodies. It is a bodiless aesthetics, a fiction fabricated out of tempered and filtered *aistheta*. It calls for a "*pensiero debole*" (Vattimo), in which simulacra of subjects exchange simulacra of objects (Baudrillard), on the sole, "democratic" condition that the "conversation" not be shackled in any way (Rorty).

There are signs that philosophy too is infected by the poison of aesthetics, to the point of hoping to find a remedy in aesthetics for its deception. From aesthetics, it would draw the consolation of keeping contact with reality. If reality is becoming aesthetic, philosophy will engage in aesthetics, or even turn itself into aesthetics, and so remain the daughter of its time.

Philosophy must remember, however, that all this is pure foolishness. First of all, because philosophy is never anything more than a bastard daughter. Premature or belated, it is always a morganatic offspring, and it is rare for its time period to acknowledge itself as its father. And it is right. No more than Rembrandt's painting, Spinoza's thought is not the offspring of the Dutch seventeenth century. Just as much as the artistic, the philosophical is irreducible to the cultural.

On the other hand, if the reality of the present time is becoming unreal in a generalized imaginary, how could philosophy become its daughter? By aestheticizing itself? But philosophical aesthetics, after having delineated the idealities of the true, the good, and the beautiful, isolated the latter and dedicated to it a discipline of thought distinct from those required by the other idealities. Contemporary culture immerses those idealities and drowns their distinctiveness in the soup of aestheticization. Philosophy, it seems, ought not to plunge in turn into that soup, it ought on the contrary to exert the power of discernment over that simplifying confusion, without forgetting to ask how to exert this power today.

Finally, the first motive traditional philosophy ought to have for objecting to aesthetics is that it cannot ignore the intrinsic "inconsistency" of the latter with regard to argumentative discourse. The "distinct discipline of thought" I just mentioned, the one required by the examination of taste, has put up such a resistance, since the beginning of philosophical aesthetics, to the ascendancy of the *logos* that it has shaken up the latter's dominion. If philosophy ought to convert itself to aesthetics, or worse, into aesthetics, the expectation must be that it will be obliged to abandon its privilege of rational knowledge. Far from reflecting the ambient aestheticization upon itself, philosophy ought to pursue further and work out more precisely the "disastrous" effects that have taken place within its core for the past two centuries under the agency of philosophical aesthetics. Philosophy thus brings philosophical aesthetics to an end by accomplishing it.

It suffices to recall briefly the difficulties inherent in philosophical aesthetics. It finds its place in modern thought, in the company of art criticism, at the moment when art begins to represent itself as an activity in itself, irreducible to the cultural and political finalities that had always and everywhere governed it. The first public exhibitions opened at the beginning of the eighteenth century. Musical, visual, and literary canons, more or less fixed by classical or Christian poetics, legitimated works intended to move court society and the community of the faithful, each of these being formed in terms of these canons. These canons defined *manners* founded upon such and such a conception of ideal beauty (which were also conceptions of the good).

On the contrary, the new public of exhibitions and salons is an unknown in the matter of taste. It comes to judge works without having been educated to bend its pleasure according to rules. It does not much believe in idealities. If, then, there are conditions of pleasure procured by art, these conditions are not rules a priori that provide norms for taste, they can be nothing more than regularities to be extracted from a multiplicity of judgments given in freedom. Aesthetics is born of this reversal that eliminates poetics, and straightaway it encounters the aporia that corners its status as a philosophical discipline: that of arguing the conditions for a judgment of taste that ought not to be determinable by a concept.

Either these conditions are in effect determinable; then taste is determined, and we return to the old regime of poetics. Or else, taste is not determined; then aesthetics cannot be argued, and the sentiment of the beautiful remains plunged in the night of intuition where all judgments are of equal value, just as all cows there are black. Kantian critique works out this fatal alternative under the rubric of the antinomy of taste. But to resolve this antinomy, the critique must acknowledge some logical monsters: a finality with no representation of the final cause, a universality with no concept, a necessity that is only exemplary, and above all, a pleasure devoid of interest. For lack of bending to these paradoxes, aesthetics falls on one side or the other, either banished from or taken hostage by argumentative discourse. It remains that, from the precarious threshold on which it stands, aesthetics denies the mere concept the power to determine the sentiment of the beautiful. Barely born, it refuses to allow rationalist philosophy the hope of tying together the whole of experience in a unitary system.

An enigma can yet be resolved, but a mystery remains impenetrable to reason. The beauty of a form is an enigma for the understanding. But for one to be able to be moved by the "presence" to the senses of a "thing" that the senses cannot present in the shape of forms is a mystery inadmissible in good logic. Every description of the sentiment of the sublime converges, however, on this aberration. The regularities of nature break down, perception fails to maintain its field, and it is admitted since Longinus that this disaster of *aisthesis* can occasion the most intense aesthetic emotions. A sentiment of aesthetics at the limit, the sublime spasm is felt, like the good fortune of taste, on the occasion of a sentiment. But this is from the fact that the latter exceeds sensibility and ravishes it to the point of loss, instead of echoing the sweet consent by which it is offered to the beautiful.

No *techne* of course can obtain this effect of *Ueber-schwengliche*, and art that aims to be sublime is doomed to the ridiculous. As for nature, it arouses this emotion only on the condition of denaturing itself. There is therefore no poetics of the sublime. Does it even have an aesthetics? The sublime calls instead on a negative ontology. That does not prevent the following absurdity to be expected of the arts: that they bear witness in the sensible (the visual, the literary, the musical . . .) to the fact that something is missing in the sensible or surpasses it—its name doesn't matter, it's the unnameable.

This expectation is not just addressed to those works the art historian calls "avant-garde." Or else, all "great" works belong to the avant-garde. For the motive of the perenniality resides in the aporia of this immaterial "presence" suggested by their matter. The modern avant-gardes have done nothing more than recall this. Once their "cultural context" has disappeared, if the works sometimes keep the living power to move us, we of course form that public with no determined taste that modernity has authorized; but above all it's because, through the "manners" of their times, these works call upon the mysterious "presence" that is of no particular time and that they countersign in the sensible. Never the same, they all strike up a single lament: aesthetic existence must incessantly be awoken from servitude and death. The alerting to nothingness is always heard in a masterpiece.

It is a philosophical banality to oppose the false plenitude of appearance to the truth of Being in its absence.

That's why philosophy gets touchy about the stubbornness of the aesthetic sentiment in its obstinate attachment to illusion. But then philosophy reduces sensation to a mode of cognition whose futility it easily demonstrates. But sensation is also the affection that "the subject"—one should say: the body/thought, which I shall call: *anima*—feels on the occasion of a sensible event. True or false, *aisthesis* immediately modifies the *anima*, displacing its disposition (its *hexis*) in the direction of well-being or ill-being. Philosophical aesthetics allows this connection as a principle. This principle, however, presupposes a substance-soul with the faculty of being affected. This metaphysical presupposition will be "placed in parentheses" in the course of the following considerations.

Philosophical aesthetics is able to see in this spontaneous affectability of the soul by the sensible the sign of an originary concordance between thought and the world. And philosophy has sometimes thought it could found on this harmony the principle of a teleology of nature being sensible for the mind. This is to make nothing of the ambivalence of sensation, which the analyses of the sublime sentiment—itself so contradictory— have nonetheless unpacked.

The affectability of the soul by sensation is not just the sign of a connivance between the two. More secretly, it conceals an absolute dependency of each in relation to the other. The *anima* exists only as affected. Sensation, whether likable or detestable, also announces to the *anima* that it would not even be, that it would remain inanimate, had nothing affected it. This soul is but the awakening of an affectability, and this remains disaffected in the absence of a timbre, a color, a fragrance, in the absence of the sensible event that excites it. This soul does not affect itself, it is only affected by the other, from the "outside." Here, existing is not the fact of a conscience aiming at its noematic correlative nor that of a permanent substance. Existing is to be awoken from the nothingness of disaffection by something sensible over there. An affective cloud lifts at that moment and deploys its nuance for a moment.

Sensation makes a break in an inert nonexistence. It alerts, it should be said, it *exists* it. What we call life proceeds from a violence exerted from the outside on a lethargy. The *anima* exists only as forced. The *aistheton* tears the inanimate from the limbo in which it inexists, it pierces its vacuity with its thunderbolt, it makes a soul emerge out of it. A sound, a scent, a color draw the pulsing of a sentiment out of the neutral continuum, out of the vacuum.

The soul comes into its existence dependent on the sensible, thus violated, humiliated. The aesthetic condition is enslavement to the *aistheton*, without which it is anesthesia. Either it is awakened by the astonishment of the other, or annihilated. The quality of the sentiment, its quiddity, well-being, ill-being, or both, might make this condition forgotten, but it cannot suppress it. Even in its most lively exaltations, the soul remains moved, excited by something outside, and it remains without autonomy. Precarious, unprepared, like the sensible event that awakes it. Even while the event brings the soul to life, casts it into the living heart of pain and/or pleasure, no matter how carried away it might be, the soul remains caught between the terror of its impending death and the horror of its servile existence. What if the *aistheton* turned out to be missing? Oh! would that the *aistheton* end up missing and that we would be done with it! In the secrecy of the soul's concert with the sensible, the affliction due to this *double bind* subsists. The aesthetic condition so described is not without analogy to the antinomic texture of the sublime sentiment, as recognized by all its analysts, and especially Burke and Kant, since Longinus. The present description extends the import of the specific analysis of the sublime sentiment to all aesthetic sentiments. Being artists, writers, sometimes philosophers, contemporaries apply themselves to detecting within sensation the "presence" of what escapes sensation: something neutral, something gray, something blank "inhabits" the nuances of a sound, a chromaticism, or a voice. Should sensation escape again from this nothingness, it is threatened with being engulfed by it. In the most luxurious Bonnards and Monets, the exaltation of colors makes an appeal against blindness.

A poem retains the unspoken within its words. "To speak without having nothing to say," writes Paul Eluard in *Capitale de la douleur* (*The Capital of Grief*). The god of the invisible, says Sam Francis, a blind god, awaits the company of painters to make visible to us what he "sees." The music of John Cage is an homage paid to silence. Art is the vow the soul makes for escaping the death promised to it by the sensible, but in celebrating in this same sensible what drags the soul out of nonexistence. Burke exactly describes this *double bind*. The *anima* is threatened with privation: speech, light, sound, life would be absolutely lacking. That's *terror*. Suddenly, the threat is lifted, the terror suspended, it's *delight*. Art, writing give grace to the soul condemned to the penalty of death, but in such a way as not to forget it.

Today's "modernity" does not expect the *aisthesis* to give the soul the peace of lovely consent, but precisely that it snatch it out of nothingness. Compare the yellows of van Gogh's *Field of Wheat* with the one used by Vermeer to temper the wall of the city of Delft. In two centuries, and whatever the case might be with the theme of the sublime, the nihilist problematics from which it proceeds is diffused into every treatment, literary and artistic, of the sensible. Nihilism does not just end the efficiency of the great narratives of emancipation, it does not just lead to the loss of values and the death of God, which render metaphysics impossible. It casts suspicion on the data of aesthetics. The *aistheton* is an event; the soul exists only if that event stimulates it; when it is lacking, the soul is dissipated into the nothingness of the inanimate. Works of art are charged with honoring this miraculous and precarious condition. Timbre, idiom, nuance are not solicited for their face value, for the immediate sense the body and culture grant them. They must be the burnt-out witnesses of an imminent and "delayed" disaster, as Marcel Duchamp used to say. And there is no poetics for regulating the manner of bearing witness, nor an aesthetics to tell how it should be received.

The *aistheta* are to the soul what the beasts of Lascaux are to the man who painted them. He lives by eating them, he perishes if they are lacking. But the painter of walls is not the eater of flesh. Nor the eye that feasts on the colors. He is the eye that renders to color the soul he owes it and that takes the soul back from it. The painterly gaze is a vision of the absence of sensation in its presence, of the *fort* in the *da*.

The sensible opus is analogous to the sexual exercise carried out by Freud's grandson on the edge of his cradle. The shuttle at the end of the string is, of course, a simulacrum of his mother. But, like in Lascaux, what is played out by the set-up matters more than what is figured in it. The child makes the object disappear over the edge by mumbling "*fort*" and celebrates its return with a "*da*." What is played out is the mutation of sight into vision and appearance into apparition. Apparition is appearance stamped with the seal of its disappearance. Art puts death's insignia on the sensible. It ravishes sensation from the night and impresses the seal of darkness upon it.

Freud somewhere confesses that he cannot define "the sexual," but that neither can he deny it. The soul is sexual like it is sensible, it exists only as subjugated to a transferential object and haunted by its defection. In the child's game, this object, like the *aistheton* in the game of art, is brought to its apparitional truth. Suspended on the edge between presence and absence, the infallible despot of the soul shows it its failure. By drawing the line of a threshold, art distinguishes itself from a symptom. The eye that paints by the sooty torchlight in

Lascaux removes the colors from the bright daylight in which they give themselves straightforwardly. He banishes them and calls on them to return transmuted. This refractive gesture traces a bordering. The latter is not a frame (which appears late in the history of painting), it is the style, it inhabits and signs the whole opus, in the entirety of its space-time. The style does not separate the soul from its existence subjugated to the sensible, it casts doubt upon the latter's self-evidence. It puts the sensible in opposition to itself, and, thereby, it puts the soul that consents, already dormant to appearances, in opposition to the soul that is awakening to apparition and that quakes.

It is understood that these few observations owe everything to works of art and almost nothing to the various "aesthetic" disciplines. That there is something anaesthetic in aesthetics is a lesson that the arts are the first to give us. And if avant-garde works have a certain privilege in this regard, it's as I've said, because they fulfill the nihilism inherent in the artistic gesture more manifestly—at least, for us—than others. Their object is the style itself. Is there any need to remark that the ascesis required by the style is at opposite poles from the complacency to manner that characterizes contemporary culture? Their only common motif is nihilism. But the cultural consists in concealing, the artistic is elaborating.

On the basis of this decision, the question raised, which is not a new one, is whether philosophy produces a work. Philosophizing is not a cultural activity, of course. After Socrates, it's writing. But what about style in philosophical writing? Is it ever addressed to the *anima*? Even the most stylized of philosophical writings, the Platonic dialogue, explicitly impugns the homage art renders the sensible. If philosophical writing happens to submit itself to the exigency of style, it is said that it is in spite of itself. This lapsus gives a sign that the body/thought, split from the mind/thought, works on the latter and resists it.

Aesthetics would be an actual part of philosophy were the *aisthesis* to stop appearing in philosophical discourse as a symptom it ignores. And it's not sufficient, to get there, that this discourse recognize its amnesia; it must work through the resistance that, in its own articulation, puts *animus* in opposition to *anima*. Now, the obsession with reasoning cannot be worked through or cured by reasoning. Nor by unreasoning. The appearance of words and their linkages must be separated from their apparition. The ascesis of style is what exerts this separation. In no way do I conclude from this that the actuality of aesthetics would require the philosopher to become an artist in writing, that is, a poet. On the contrary, it matters that between poem and matheme, as Alain Badiou says, or rather in the webs woven by each other, a reflective writing insists on questioning its propriety, and on that very account, to expropriate itself endlessly.

Finally, do we have to add this in order to forewarn of an interpretative error? These few considerations bear only on the *anima minima, that* affect born of *this* sensible apparition, blow by blow. I call this soul minimal because, as the minimal condition of aesthetics, it is

taken in its strictest comprehension. It has been represented without continuity, without memory, and without mind (neither images nor ideas) in order to get the
closest possible fix on the mystery of sensation: a given
sensible material (a sound, a scent, etc., to which we
join, provisionally and with reservations, the word and
the sentence, if it is true that literature deals with them
as the matter of language), a given sensible material
awakening an affect. "A brief feeling is born from an
event, itself issuing forth from nothing"; only an *archi-
épochè* of sensation could perhaps enunciate this proposition. It would suspend not only the prejudgments of
the world and of substance but also those of subjectivity
and of life.

To the severity of this suspension, let me add in
closing a temperament. The minimal soul, I said, is to
be thought as being without memory. But that may be
excessive, or at least, it asks to be specified. The soul
awakened, *existed* by the sensible does not of course
know its past, in the sense that thought focuses on an
object from long ago to reactualize it. But when the
sensible has undergone the artistic gesture of annihilation by which its appearance is transformed into an apparition, the momentary affect it awoke instantly bears
with it the value of a return. What comes back in this
time to come is not located in the time of clocks and
consciences, and is not worth remembering. The relation must be reversed: what is to come comes forth as a
coming back. That's why the gesture always induces a
nostalgia and motivates an amnesia.

Sources

The texts of this collection have been modified to a greater or a lesser extent from their original publication in the following works and under the following titles. (All texts previously published in English have been retranslated after consultation with the published version.—Trans.)

1. "Marie in Japan," trans. David Palumbo-Liu, *Stanford Literature Review* 10 (Spring 1993).

2. "Zone," Actes du colloque "Le philosophe dans la cité" (May 1992), *Les Cahiers de philosophie* (Fall 1993).

3. "Intriguer, ou le paradoxe du graphiste," in *Vive les graphistes!* exhibit catalog, Centre Georges Pompidou, September-October 1990 (Paris: Syndicat national des graphistes, 1990).

4. "Qui perd gagne?" *Cahiers Antwerpen 1993*, no. 0: *Discours et littérature: sur l'intéressant* (Antwerp, 1993).

5. "The Wall, the Gulf and the Sun," extracts, trans. T. Cochran and J.-F. Lyotard, in Marc Poster, ed., *Politics, Theory and Contemporary Culture* (New York: Columbia University Press, 1993).

6. "Eine postmoderne Fabel," trans. Silvia Henke, in J. Huber,

ed., *Wahrnehmung der Gegenwart* (Zurich: Museum für Gestaltung, 1992).

7. "La terre n'a pas de chemins par elle-même," preface to the Japanese edition of *Heidegger et "les juifs,"* ed. and trans. Kunio Honma (Tokyo: Fujiwara, 1993).

8. "Ligne générale," in C. Evrard, ed., *Librement dit, Écrits sur les droits de l'homme* (Paris: Cherche Midi, 1991).

9. "Aller et retour," extracts, introduction to John Rajchman and Cornel West, eds., *La Pensée américaine contemporaine*, trans. Andrée Lyotard-May (Paris: PUF, 1991), French translation of *The Post-Analytic Philosophy* (New York: Columbia University Press, 1985).

10. "Foreword," trans. Andrew Benjamin, in Andrew Benjamin, ed., *The Lyotard Reader* (London: Basil Blackwell, 1988).

11. "Pour une 'ontologie' du musée imaginaire," Actes du colloque "La nouvelle Alexandrie," May 1993, Collège international de philosophie, Programme de recherche en muséologie, Direction des Musées de France, forthcoming.

12. "A l'insu," in Nicole Loraux and M. Olender, eds., *Politiques de l'oubli* (Paris: Seuil, 1988); previous English translation by G. Van Den Abbeele and James Creech in Miami Theory Collective, *Community at Loose Ends* (Minneapolis: University of Minnesota Press, 1991).

13. "Terror on the Run," trans. Philipp Wood, Proceedings of conference on "Terror and Consensus," April 1993, Department of French Studies, Rice University, forthcoming.

14. "Musique, mutique," in Christine Buci-Glucksman and M. Lévinas, eds., *L'Idée musicale* (Paris: Presses universitaires de Vincennes, 1993).

15. "Anima minima," trans. M. Kalbe and Charles Pries, in W. Welsch, ed., *Aktualität des Aesthetischen* (Munich: Fink Verlag, 1993).

Index

Abraham, 77
Académie française, 179
Adorno, Theodor, 23
aesthetics, 10, 24–32, 52, 101, 130–32, 166, 178–79, 206, 207, 214, 231–33, 235–37, 242–49; and art criticism, 50–51, 166, 181, 238–39; and graphic art, 33–47; periodization, 217–18; relation to philosophy, 237–42, 247. *See also* Constructivism; sublime; Suprematism
Ainu, 103, 108, 110
Alexander the Great, 57, 164
Alexandria, 18, 163–64, 168
allography, 155–56, 158, 162
Altdorfer, Albrecht, 8
America, 105, 111; philosophy in, 123–47; and the American dream, 201
Amnesty International, 119
Amsterdam, 19

Anglophones, 153–54, 162
Apollinaire, Guillaume, 18, 206
Arendt, Hannah, 187
Aristotle, 11, 96, 125–26, 127, 133, 227
Artaud, Antonin, 204
Athens, 201
Augustine, Saint, Bishop of Hippo, 96, 213; *Confessions*, 206
autography, 170, 171, 176–78, 180

Bach, Johann Sebastian, 229
Badiou, Alain, 248
Baghdad, 76
Balzac, Jean-Louis Guez de, 19
Barcelona, 47
Barrès, Maurice, 172
Barthes, Roland, 215
Baudelaire, Charles, 18, 208–9, 212–14
Baudrillard, Jean, 237

Jean-François Lyotard is one of the principal French philosophers and intellectuals of the twentieth century. Best known for his analyses of postmodernism, Lyotard is the author of numerous works, which include *The Postmodern Condition* (1984), *Just Gaming* (1985), *The Differend: Phrases in Dispute* (1988), *Heidegger and "the jews"* (1990), *The Postmodern Explained* (1992), and *Political Writings* (1993), all published by the University of Minnesota Press. Lyotard is professor emeritus at the University of Paris and a professor in the Department of French and Italian at Emory University.

Georges Van Den Abbeele is a professor of French and director of the Davis Humanities Institute, Critical Theory Program, and Humanities Program at the University of California, Davis. He is the translator of Jean-François Lyotard's *The Differend: Phrases in Dispute* (1988), and the author of *Travel as Metaphor* (1992), both published by the University of Minnesota Press. Van Den Abbeele is currently completing a book tentatively titled *Utopias of Difference: For a Genealogy of the French Intellectual*.